The History of Borough Fen Decoy

by
TONY COOK and R.E.M. PILCHER

WITH A FOREWARD BY SIR PETER SCOTT, CBE, DSC,

ILLUSTRATIONS BY ANNE TREADWELL-COOK

FIRST PUBLISHED 1982

PROVIDENCE PRESS, WARDY HILL, ELY, CAMBS.

ISBN 0-903803-08-9

Printed by FORUM·PRINT Ltd.   Designed by J.A. COX

Contents

FRONT COVER

Looking into SE pipe, note wing poles and landing near entrance

[photo: Anne Treadwell-Cook]

Foreword

On 5th March 1932 my then new-found farmer friend, Will Tinsley of Holbeach, took me to Borough Fen Decoy for the first time. There I met Billy Williams, the decoyman who showed me a secret and fascination place, which in those days still had sinister consequences for thousands of wild ducks each winter. The 17-acre wood hid a small pond of 2½ acres with 8 curved and tapering ditches called 'pipes', covered by string netting on hoops and fringed with reed screens. The ducks were first enticed into these pipes and then driven into a detachable 'tunnel net' at the narrow end.

I became determined that the ducks should not be killed and sent to market, but rather ringed and released to add to our knowledge of their migratory journeys. The objective was finally achieved, though not for many years and the intervention of the Second World War.

But from the day of my first visit I was fascinated by the techniques used for catching the ducks, and by the way they had been evolved in Holland and England in the 17th and 18th centuries. The word 'decoy', which is now so widely used to denote enticement by delusion, is derived from two Dutch words - **eende**, meaning ducks and **kooi**, meaning cage or trap. So **eende-kooi** is what such places are called in the Netherlands. It may be that, when the word was anglicised, **een** was recognised as the Dutch indefinite article and it was then supposed that the device must be **een dekooi** - or a 'decoy'. One of the techniques for catching ducks in a decoy involves training tame ducks to respond to the decoyman's whistle and because initially they lived in the decoy they were 'decoy ducks' - or, for short, 'decoys'.

'Decoys' could also be used to attract wild ducks for shooting, and sham ones were found to be effective, which led to a long tradition of carved wooden decoys, and inflatable rubber and plastic decoys. Then, too, the meaning was extended to include human subterfuge in peace and war.

Duck decoys by the nature of their operations must be quiet places free from overt disturbances, and once the requirement to send dead ducks to market has been superceded by the scientific objective of marking and releasing the birds, a decoy can become a genuine sanctuary, not only for the ducks but for all the other creatures that live within its confines or visit it seasonally.

By 1954 all killing of ducks in Borough Fen Decoy had ceased and the place had become a sanctuary. Peace had been declared.

The historical and antiquarian interest of this ancient decoy has now been recorded by the authors, who have been my close friends for very many years. It is therefore a particular pleasure to be contributing this foreward to the book.

6 January 1981

Preface

In 1960 the Council of the Wildfowl Trust, who had recently obtained from the owners a lease of Borough Fen Decoy, decided to open it for a few days to the public. The response was good and the practice has been continued each year ever since.

Visitors are given a pamphlet which gives a brief history of the decoy and something of the technique and purpose of catching ducks. Amongst the visitors have been ornithologists, entomologists and antiquaries, the last anxious to know something of an industry that at one time flourished so healthily in the Fens. It seemed to the present authors that the pamphlet served to stimulate interest and the asking of questions rather than the satisfying of them and that this could only be done by means of a book.

The history of duck decoys and the technique of catching ducks in them has been given with a clarity and detail which cannot be surpassed by Sir Ralph Payne-Gallway in *The Book of Duck Decoys*. Although the book was published nearly a century ago in 1886, there has been little change in the art and practice of decoying and only a small change in the materials used in that practice. The book is, however, now rare and expensive and not readily accessible.

1. In the Decoy

The decoyman got out of the Land Rover, unlocked the gates of the decoy and drove in. He had been out that morning and had collected a load of tail corn given him by a friendly farmer when he had finished threshing. He unloaded the sacks, carrying them into the shed. It was a pity to leave them out in the rain to spoil and, since the ducks were getting stale and taking no notice of the dog, he would have to rely more and more on feeding the pipes if he was to keep on catching ducks. His dog, Piper, sniffed at a rat-hole. A fresh one, the decoyman thought to himself; they had finished getting the beet up in the nearby fields and the rats which had lived and bred amongst the beet during the summer had been driven to find shelter elsewhere. Far too many were finding shelter in the decoy but he was getting on top of them.

With the last bag of corn stored in the shed, he walked to his hut, collected a couple of empty sacks and walked along the path. There had been a lot of fog lately, as he expected in November, and the ducks after leaving the decoy had often failed to find it again at first light, and so the numbers had gone down. Two days ago there had been less than two hundred ducks on the pond, but last night it had rained and the wind had got up. When he had looked at the pond at dawn that morning there were clearly many more ducks there than the night before and now, as he looked up, five more Mallard came in. At first, very high up, they flew over the pond and then with a slight flicker of their wings and a perceptible pause, they swung round in three wide circles, losing height rapidly and then, suddenly, they plummeted down the last thirty feet and alighted on the pond.

1

Were these old birds, he wondered, that had lost their way on one of those foggy mornings and had now found their way in again, or were they birds that had come to the decoy last winter and at last found it again? They had certainly come down very confidently as though they knew the place but strange birds will do that if they catch sight of their own kind in numbers and apparently at complete ease. Anyway the birds on the pond should soon be waking up, for it was nearly three o'clock, and feeling hungry. With any luck he should make a catch.

He walked along the path until he came to the track leading to the look-out, the old log cabin, from where he could see into most of the pipes and all the pond. He walked up the track, lifted the sack curtain which acted as a door and went in. He peeped through the slats in the wall and out over the pond. On his right there were twenty or more Teal perched on an old ash tree that had half fallen into the water. Below, a duck Mallard was trying to incite a couple of drakes. Wait until after Christmas, he thought, and it will be a different story. The duck, tired of making ineffectual gestures to unresponsive drakes, jumped out of the water onto the ash tree trunk, bundling off a drake Teal into the water. It rose and settled on what was little more than a twig with the ease of any perching bird. Out on the pond there were many more Mallard and several more Teal than there had been yesterday. There were still several ducks in the reed beds and he could not say what the total count might be. He would wait until dusk when they all flew out and then he would have a better idea. He could hear a duck Wigeon calling but he could not hear or see any drakes. There were five Shovelers out in the middle, swimming and sifting the surface water through their bills. There was still a fair amount of duck-weed in the dykes and some had flowed in when he topped up the pond from the sluice a week ago.

There were several ducks swimming round the mouth of the pipes and across on the other side of the pond, in the south-east pipe, he could see ducks well past the first hoop. He should be able to catch these by ''showing'' at the head show place.

There was little wind and he must walk very quietly. He stooped to pick up two broken twigs that had come down in last night's wind. If he had trodden on those, the sound would certainly have alerted the ducks. With his dog at his heels he crept silently to the show place and showed himself suddenly from behind the first screen. As soon as they saw him the ducks jumped into the air but the three nearest him, near the first hoop, broke back and flew onto the pond. The others flew up the pipe. He ran past the screens driving two swimming ducks in front of him; the others had flown on and already reached the tunnel net. He pulled out the first hoop from between its stakes and gave the net a twist, so closing the net, and gathered up the slack. He laid the net down and started to take the ducks out, putting them in one of his sacks. There were twenty-one Mallard, nine ducks and twelve drakes. He picked up the sacks and with his dog at his heels, walked to the next pipe. He looked through a hole in the screen. Several Mallard were, he saw, swimming near the mouth of the pipe and might follow the dog in.

He put the dog over a dog leap a little way up the pipe and watched the ducks. They stopped swimming and stayed quite still, their necks outstretched and looking intently up the pipe. He put the dog over again and the ducks, straining to see what the rapidly disappearing object was, started to swim towards it. He put the dog over a third and fourth time, at first rather further away and then nearer. After swimming just within the first hoop they started to swim round in circles. He could see that they were losing interest and were not to be taken that way. Softly whistling his dog to heel he started to walk back towards his hut. Presently the dog left him to go a short distance into the undergrowth where a rabbit had died recently of myxomatosis. There had been another outbreak and now there did not seem to be a live rabbit left in the decoy. Perhaps it was a good thing. Rabbits were a nuisance; they made holes in the tunnel nets unless one wired them off and it was surprising through what a small hole a Teal could escape. They nibbled, too, at the osier sets and killed them off by eating away the bark. All the same, it would be a pity if they all went for he liked to see the odd one about. It was strange how they managed to get in after building such a good wire boundary fence, well sunk in, all round the decoy. At least it kept the foxes out; foxes were much more of a nuisance; they disturbed the birds and spoilt the dogging.

Back at the hut he put the sacks down and got out his rule and calipers for measuring the birds, and his rings and pliers, and sat down at his desk to record the details of the birds he had just caught. Telling the sex at this time of the year was easy enough but it was often difficult to say whether they were young or old and sometimes he had to compromise by calling them full-grown. He put a ring on one leg and made sure that it was secure and fitted well and then recorded the number on it. He measured the bill, wing and tarsus of each bird and, when he had done this, released it through the open window. Piper, with muffled cries of excitement, pranced round the window as each bird was released. The old fool, the decoyman thought, how many hundreds of ducks have you seen me let go and you still get excited. He did not want any Mallard for orientation release experiments. He wished he could catch more Teal, it was difficult to get enough to try out under all conditions of cloud cover and sunshine to satisfy the scientists. He put away his gear and left the hut.

It was now getting dusk and he could see the first evening star as he looked up in the sky. It did not look as though there would be fog

3

that night, more likely it would freeze. When he reached the track he walked up again to the look-out. The ducks, he could see, were now mostly all out in the middle of the pond and very wide awake. He sat there watching. He could feel behind and beside him, as he had felt so many times before, the friendly ghosts of previous decoymen, all members of the Williams family who had worked the decoy for so many, many years before him. He was not alarmed by them, he liked their company and to feel that they were there. They had all done the same job as he and had had the same interests. He never turned round to see if they really were there; that would have spoiled it all, but sometimes he thought his dog saw them.

Presently the ducks started to leave the pond, at first only a few at a time and often a single bird would fly off in great haste, trying to overtake others that had left a short time before. Everywhere ducks were on the water, their outstretched necks moving rapidly backwards and forwards, a sure sign that they were about to take off. Soon there was a general movement and all the remaining ducks took wing, almost together, and the pond was empty. There must have been, he thought, about eight hundred birds, nearly three hundred of them Teal and a few Shovelers. He never saw the Wigeon go off, perhaps it went with the big lot of Mallard.

He left the look-out and went back to the hut. He had a quick look round, tidied away a few papers and then closed the door behind him. He locked the decoy gates and drove home along the dyke side. As he drove, his mind turned once more to the ghosts he had left behind him in the decoy. What manner of men were these famous old Williams family of decoymen? Although they would find so much changed in the outside world, they would probably find little changed inside their decoy and he used many of their ways of doing things, taught him by the last of their long line. He would love to see this same countryside teeming with wildfowl as they knew it, and to learn from their own lips something of their way of life.

2. The Rise and Subsequent Decline of Duck Decoys in the Fens

Borough Fen Decoy in the Parish of Newborough, a few miles north of Peterborough, lies about half way along the Western border of the largest plain in England, the Fenland.Although not the earliest of the decoys in Britain it enjoys the distinction of being the oldest to remain in continuous use since its first construction. Nearby in the surrounding fenland there were at one time many such decoys. Eight miles away in Deeping Fen there were five, four within a mile of one another. In Bourne and in Cowbit Fens and to the east of Fleet Fen three decoys flourished. In South Lincolnshire alone there were nearly forty at one time, all making a good profit for their owners. All these have now gone. Sometimes a name on a map, such as Decoy Farm, survives as a reminder of their former existence. Occasionally a small spinney remains, a relic of the old decoy wood or an old pond with its pipes may be recognised under a tangle of bramble and scrub. More frequently all traces have gone, removed by the plough, and corn, potatoes and sugar beet grow where the old decoy stood.

In order to understand the conditions which made the construction of decoys not only possible but also highly profitable, and to appreciate the changes which led to their ultimate almost complete disappearance, one must know something of the early history of the Fens, the nature of the land and the character and occupations of the inhabitants. Although many factors, largely economic, played their part in their prosperity and in their fall, their rise was almost wholly governed by the state of the drainage of the Fens. Since this is a book about Borough Fen, only the history of the neighbouring fenlands will be discussed.

Before the Romans came to Britain much of the fenland was densely wooded. The familiar bog oaks, which are still brought to light by the plough, are relics of the ancient woodland. At the time of the Roman occupation the Fens were much drier than they were, for instance, in the seventeenth century. Although there were large areas of marsh, inland lakes and meres, much of the country, notably south of Spalding, grew crops of corn. The Romans did much efficient and wisely planned drainage, particularly in the north and west, but probably no great drainage system was required then. Gradually, however, the land, at one time much above sea level, sank as the peat dried out. The rivers, which had now lost their fall, silted up at their mouths. The water, especially in winter, could not get away fast enough and flowed over the banks. Marshes and meres became inland seas, and with the lowered level of the land the countryside was subject to inundation by the sea itself. At times, and almost every year in winter, the only habitable places were the small islands of higher ground which rose from the surrounding swamps.

Probably the most colourful pictures of the neighbouring fenland in the Dark Ages are those when St. Guthlac, a youth of the royal line of Mercia, having shaved off his long hair, the mark of his royal blood, retired to the Fens and founded at Crowland his solitary cell. The very name Crowland is said to mean crude and muddy land. Ingulph, the biographer of St. Guthlac, gives his impression of the Fens at the beginning of the eighth century. "There is", he writes, "in the middle of Britain a hideous fen of huge bigness, which, beginning at the banks of the River Grante, extends itself from the south to the north in a very long tract, even to the sea; oftimes clouded with moist and dark vapours, having within it divers islands and woods, as also crooked and winding rivers". Ingulph goes on to describe how St. Guthlac found "in the desert places in the vast wilderness one Tatwine, who took him by boat to a certain remote island in the secret part of the lake, to a place called Croyland, known only to a few, for no countrymen could endure to live in it, by reason that such apparitions of devils were frequently seen there". St. Guthlac soon became familiar with these devils which were, no doubt apparitions seen in the delirium of "Fen ague", malaria, for so long endemic in the Fens. Ingulph's description is not without prejudice, for it must be remembered that the greater the miseries and hardships his hero had to bear, the greater his piety.

The foundation of the cell by St. Guthlac was to have a profound influence on local history and development. After fifteen years of solitude St. Guthlac died and Aethelbald, King of Mercia, founded in his memory the monastery of Crowland. The foundation was endowed with a grant of land on the borders of which lay Borough Fen. The monks were given a charter to build a town with a right of common land for themselves and their servants. The Charter is dated 716 A.D. Meanwhile at Peakirk, Pega sister to St. Guthlac, had founded her cell. A monastery had already been founded at Peterborough (Medehamstead) in 655, and some fifty years after the foundation at Crowland, a company of monks had established themselves at Thorney. These monasteries had been founded intentionally in what was considered the meanest and most miserable part of the kingdom, but by the wealth they attracted and the order they established they exerted a remarkable influence on the neighbouring fens.

Although attacked and destroyed by the Danes and later by the Normans at the time of the Conquest, Crowland Abbey survived and indeed prospered. Successive Abbots were able to improve the surrounding countryside. In the eleventh century Abbot Egelric so improved the marshes around Crowland as to be able to plough and sow them, and he was able to supply the whole countryside with corn. At the same time also, according to Dugdale, "Richard de Rulos, The King's Chamberlain, being much given to husbandry, such as tillage and the breeding of cattle, took in a great part of Deeping Fen and converted it into meadow and pasture. He also enclosed the river Welland by a mighty bank and by erecting on that bank divers tenements and cottages, did, in a short time, make it a large town".

The Fens at this time and in the following century appear to have presented a much more pleasing picture than they did at the time of St. Guthlac. Henry of Huntingdon, writing of a visit he made in the summer of 1287, says "This fenny country is very pleasant and agreeable to the eye, watered by the many rivers which run through it, diversified by many large and small lakes and adorned with many roads and islands". William of Malmesbury wrote of the same period "There is such an abundance of fish as to cause amazement to strangers, while natives laugh at their surprise. Waterfowl are so plentiful that persons can not only assuage their hunger with both sorts of food, but can eat to satisfy for a penny". This land of plenty had, however, its dangers and disasters. On New Year's Day after that very year, according to Stowe's Chronicle, "As well by the vehemency of the wind as the violence of the sea, the monasteries of Spalding and many churches were over-thrown and destroyed. The whole of Holland in Lincolnshire was, for the most part, turned into a standing pool; so that an intolerable multitude of men, women and children were overwhelmed with water". Deeping Fen became an inland sea and Crowland an island, cut off from the rest of the country by the rising waters.

There was probably little material change in the Fens in the next two or three centuries. The land remained subject to frequent inundations, some of it drying out in summer and much of it disappearing under water in winter. In the summer the retreating waters would leave behind rich grassland for grazing and the meres, fringed with sedge and reed, would return temporarily to moderate proportions and become the home of the abundant waterfowl. These waterfowl were a natural harvest for the inhabitants to take and a special technique, in which one can see the rudiments of the classical decoy, was evolved for the gathering of it.

In John Ray's edition of F. Willughby's Ornithology (1678) the following description occurs. "In the Fens of the Isle of Ely, Norfolk, Lincolnshire and about Crowland and elsewhere, Ducks, Wigeons, Teals and other birds of this kind, at what time they moult their feathers and cannot fly, are taken yearly in great number of Nets, placed after this manner:

7

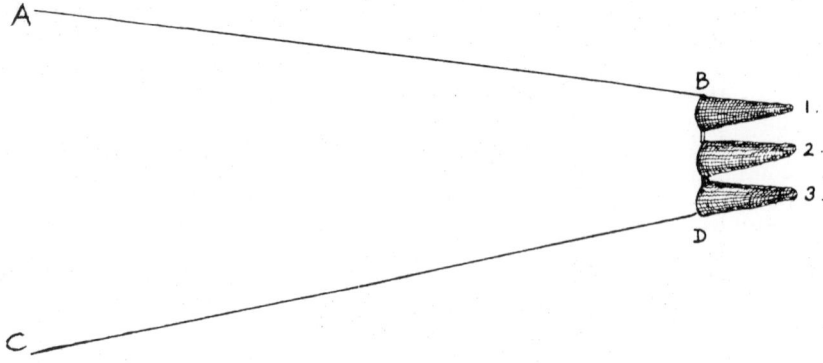

AB, CD are Nets extending a great length in the form of a wall or hedge, inclining one to another, at the further end of which, before they converge in an angle, are placed 1, 2 or 3 or more conoidal Nets, like tunnelling Nets for Partridges, which, being so prepared, and the day of fowling set, there is a great concourse of men and boats. These drive the Birds, now unable to fly, into the grounds inclosed in the Nets with long Staves and Poles, and so by degrees into those conoidal tunnels, 1, 2 and 3, disposed, as we said in the angle. By the way many are knocked down by the Boatmen and other Rabble with Poles, others and more are driven into the side Nets, AB, CD. These belong to them that own the Nets (for the Nets for the most part have several owners), those fall to their sharers who killed them. Those which are cooped up, and driven into the end tunnels, 1, 2 and 3, belong to the Lord of the Soil. To one fowling you shall have sometimes four hundred Boats meet. We have heard that there have been four thousand Mallards taken at one Drive in Deeping Fen''.

This method of catching ducks had been in use for many years. In 1432 a mob, armed with sticks and swords, took 600 wildfowl out of the Abbot's ''Decoy'' at Crowland, infringing the rights of private property. There had been previous occasions, one as early as 1280, and again in 1415, when similar raids had been the subject of litigation, but so long as the stock of wildfowl continued, the practice was a highly profitable one. Vast numbers of duck were killed in this way. Gough, in his edition of Camden, says that, about 1720, 3,000 ducks were taken in a single drive. Daniel, in his *Rural Sports,* speaks of the same number being taken in a single drive near Spalding. In the Archives of the Gentlemen's Society at Spalding an interesting document, apparently an account, survives. It is headed ''Deeping Fen Ducking'' and beneath this, ''That is, the country People have Right of Common, Enclosing hundreds of acres with large Nets having pipes at their Ends and driving the Moulted Mallards or Male Wildfowles into those Nets. N.B. There are very few female or Ducks when they being with their Young feeding out at Sea, but the Drakes being sick or unable to fly their Wing Feathers being gone with casting their Feathers stay amongst the Reeds and Rushes in the broad fresh Waters.

The Acct. of Fowle taken at the Ducking of several days in June 1728 by the People having the Right of Common,

June ye 20 = 394 dozen
June ye 21 = 387 dozen
June ye 24 = 305 dozen

Signed by Joseph Atkinson who was present and kept the Acct. for the whole Company of Duckers.

Whereof 155 dozen were taken the 1st. day being Thursday the 20th. June at One Push into the Netts''.

This vast slaughter of ducks had given rise many years previously, and on several occasions subsequently, to action by Parliament. By the Statute 25 H. VIII C.XI. 1534 ''The Cause of the Decay in Wildfowl is attributed to the taking them in Summer Time and in their Moulting Season and therefore this is thereby prohibited to be done between the last day of May and the last day of August. Spa iiid for Each Fowl''. It is doubtful if this act was ever observed very closely. With the dissolution in 1536 of the smaller monasteries and of the larger ones, including Thorney, Crowland and Peterborough in 1539, an enormous acreage of land was suddenly deprived of its traditional owners and, although fresh owners were soon found, the old allegiance was lost. The Act was in any case repealed at the ''Petition of the Fenn Men'' by 3 and 4 Ed. VI. CVII. 1550. ''It is hereby Sayed to have been found by Experience that there has been less plenty of Fowl brought to the Markets since that law had been made, and moreover it is sayed to have arisen in a Private Cause to have been of common Commodity and in some sort branded as an Impious Law''. This second Act was not repealed until Ann CCX 1710 when ''the driving or taking of Wild Fowl in ye Moulting Season between 1st. July and 1st. Septr. prohibited Spa 5d. a Fowl''. In a Royal Society letter this is explained as ''a law for the better protection of the Game & says in ye season ye Fowl are sick and their Flesh Unsavoury and Unwholesome''. In addition of a fine of 5d. for each fowl taken there was a further penalty of not less than 14 days or more than one month in prison, with whipping, hard labour and the loss of nets and engines employed.

The practice of catching ducks by driving when the old birds were in moult and the young unable to fly could only be carried out, at least openly, as long as it was legal. The fen-men were not remarkable for their respect for the law but, although surveillance was probably not very strict, even in the most out of the way places

9

Driving Waterfowl in the Sixteenth Century
from *The Book of Duck Decoys by Sir Ralph Payne-Gallewey*

it must have been very difficult to assemble the necessary number of men and to carry out the noisy manoeuvres with any degree of secrecy. It was, however, in all probability a much more material consideration than fear of the law which led to the abandonment of ducking. It was no longer profitable. Reduction by more effective drainage of the number of suitable meres, excessive driving of the few birds that remained leading to the abandonment of their traditional homes and a decrease in their number by years of slaughter made the share-out at the end of the drives so small among so many that the effort was scarcely worthwhile. Efficient drainage had now made it possible to put the land to other more regular, more profitable and lawful uses. It had also made it possible for the man who wished to continue to earn his livelihood by catching ducks to do so all the year round, save for that part forbidden by law, on land he owned or rented and without the assistance of the rabble around him.

The story of the drainage of the Fens which has played such an important part in the rise, the period of prosperity and the decline of duck decoys, even so far as it concerns the countryside around Borough Fen, can only be told briefly here. It is the story of man's battle against nature; the battle swaying first one way and then the other, with nature succeeding at first through man's ignorance and later through his incompetence or indifference, but with man

10

gradually gaining the upper hand; a battle which continues today.

With the establishment of the monasteries of Peterborough, Crowland and Thorney and the hamlets around them, the Abbots became the first drainage engineers. Their efforts were, however, entirely local and aimed at providing sufficient pasture and arable land for their own needs. They were subject to frequent interruptions at the hands of invaders such as the Danes and, later, the Normans, and they were finally brought to a standstill by the Dissolution in 1539. An enormous acreage of land was at once deprived of the only people capable of managing it. Only a few years later, in 1562, Sir William Dugdale wrote "the total drowning of this Great Level (whereof we have in our times been eye witnesses) hath, for the most part, been occasioned by the neglect of putting the laws of sewers in due execution; before the dissolution of the monasteries by King Henry VIII the passages for the water were kept with cleansing and the banks with better repair, chiefly through the care and cost of these religious houses".

In places where the influence of the monasteries had never been felt there had been little concerted effort at drainage until the 13th century. Self interest and jealousy had led to local feuds and bitterness and in 1225 the Commissioners of Sewers were granted a Charter to assist in the disputes which had appeared in Court at intervals during the preceeding years. The Commissioners showed little enthusiasm for their work and rather less efficiency. At one time the Nene, the Welland and the Great Ouse flowed through Wisbech to the sea; the Little Ouse alone flowed through Lynn. In 1292 they diverted the Great Ouse into the Little Ouse, which proved incapable of taking so much water; the Nene had now insufficient water to scour the channel and the mouth silted up. Borough Fen and Thorney were constantly flooded. Crowland fared little better for its once valuable arable land became a swamp. The villagers rang their church bells backwards as a warning against the all too common floodings.

This state of affairs continued with very little improvement for another two and a half centuries. The local inhabitants did little to help and were often actively hostile. In 1546 they cut a hole in the bank during a period of flood and many people were drowned in the inundation. The culprits were caught and hanged and their bodies placed in the breach.

Petition to the King and Privy Council followed petition but with little effect. James I made some effort to improve the situation but was met with the usual indifference, self interest or active opposition In 1619 a plan had been made to drain Deeping and several other fens. The Undertakers who were given the task deepened the outfall of the Welland and Nene with much improvement of the

11

lands but as the taxes on the land which they had been promised were never paid, they ran out of money and were forced to abandon their efforts. The Commissioners of Sewers undertook to do the work and did nothing. In 1629 Cornelius Vermuyden, a Dutchman with a wide experience in land drainage, was engaged by the Earl of Bedford and his Adventurers to undertake the drainage of Fenland. Vermuyden met with much opposition and some of his adventurers were ruined. At a Session of Sewers, held in Lynn, in 1631, an offer made by Vermuyden to carry out the drainage of Deeping Fen was accepted, but "the country being not satisfied to deal with Sir Cornelius, in regard that he was an alien, they intimated their dislike to the Commissioners". He was compelled to abandon his original plan and at his next attempt he divided the area into the North, Middle and South Levels, Borough Fen being included in the North Level. His work progressed and in 1637 at a Session of Sewers, held at St. Ives, the Level was declared "drained according to the tenor and true intent of the said Act or Law of Sewers made King's Lynn".

The task of draining Deeping Fen was finally carried out separately from the work on the Levels. The Earl of Bedford was given the concession to drain the fen and "divers gentlemen became Adventurers for the exsiccation thereof". Among these was a Dutchman, Sir Philibert Vernatt, from who Vernatt's drain, sluice and bridge received their name.

Up to the beginning of the 17th century, when the Undertakers first attempted their improvements, the Welland had divided at Crowland, one branch flowing through Spalding and thence to the sea, the other joining a branch of the Nene at No Man's Land Hirne and discharging at Cross Keys Wash. Vermuyden planned to divert the Welland and its tributary, the Glen, "which by bursting its banks, continually flooded Deeping Fen" to join the Nene, which he held to have a better outfall than the Welland, at Guyhirne. This was opposed on the grounds that "of late years during winter floods, a great part of the Welland floodwaters had forsaken their proper channel and passed through Crowland and then into Borough and Thorney Fens, and so stole to the sea by the Wisbech outfall, because the Welland was so filled with silt and sand and was not half as deep as it was made by the late Undertakers". The Adventurers widened and deepened the Welland from St. James' Deeping to Spalding and from Spalding to the outfall. In 1650 a bank, 70 ft wide at the bottom and 8 ft high was constructed by the Adventurers to give further protection to the North Level. This bank ran from Peakirk and thence to Crowland whence it passed to Brotherhouse, running half a mile north of Borough Fen Decoy, to join the Holland Bank which led to Spalding. On the north side of this bank lay Crowland and Cowbit Washes.

Sir William Dugdale says that at this time the land was so well drained that "in the summer the whole fen yielded great quantities of grass and hay and would in a short time have made winter ground, but that the country people, taking advantage of the confusion throughout the kingdom, which ensued soon after the convention of the Long Parliament, Possessed themselves thereof, so that the banks and sewers being neglected by the Adventurers, it became again overflowed". By 1700 Deeping Fen had become floodland again, only to be saved by the advent of the windmill pump. Elsewhere much of the peat land had shrunk and local floodings recurred, but by and large the fens had been well and truly drained.

But not to everyone's content; for what Dugdale (who was much prejudiced towards his "Imbanking") calls that "almost barbarous and lazy beggarly people" the fenmen, felt themselves robbed of their livelihood of fishing and fowling. "Tell them", says Fuller in his *Worthies of England,* "of the great benefit to the Publick, because where a Pike or Duck fed formerly, now a Bullock or Sheep is fattened; they will be ready to return that if they be taken in taking that Bullock or Sheep, the rich owner indicteth them for felons; whereas that Pike or Duck were their own goods, only for the pains of catching them. So impossible is it that the best project, though perfectly executed, should please all interests and affection.

A duck decoy consists essentially of a piece of water modified in various ways to make it more attractive to ducks and for the catching of them. As long as the surrounding countryside consisted of innumerable meres and ponds and was subject to frequent inundation it was difficult to make one site more attractive than another. But when more effective drainage had restricted the amount of open water without as yet reducing the number of ducks the way was open for a man owning a suitable area of water and land around it to develop it. Such a man had many advantages over his private property protected by Act of Parliament [1]. By erecting a fence he could keep intruders away and by the planting of trees and bushes he could give the birds the seclusion and sense of security they required. He could attract birds onto the pond by feeding and by a

---

[1] This was established very early on. Thomas Lloyd (see Andrew Williams, p.43) was successful in a lawsuit against a Mr. Mytton, ancestor of the notorious Jack Mytton, who had built a forge for the purpose of disturbing Mr. Lloyd's decoy. Mr. Lloyd died in 1692. In 1705 in the case of Keeble v. Hickeringall, a decoyman brought an action against another neighbouring decoyman who had wilfully disturbed his, the plaintiff's decoy, by firing shots near it. Judgement was given by Lord Chief Justice Holt in favour of the plaintiff on the grounds that "the plaintiff had learned the art of alluring wild ducks on his pond on private property, for his own pleasure and profit, as he had every right to do. That the person who made the Decoy should benefit by the skill, outlay and care requisite to construct and manage it. That the owner of a Decoy had every right to expect the law to protect him from wilful injury to it"

system of sluices he could control the level of water in his pond, preventing it from drying out in summer or flooding in the winter. Instead of catching large numbers of birds on a few meres on a few days to be shared among a number of villagers at a time when birds were out of condition and, when killed, would not keep, he could now catch ducks throughout the season permitted him by law and he could keep the proceeds of the sale of these birds for himself.

Sir Harry Spelman, who died in 1641, says "Sir W. Wodehouse (who lived in the reign of James I, 1603—25) made among us the first device for catching Ducks, known by the foreign name of koye". This was accepted by Sir Ralph Payne-Gallwey as correct and that previous mentions of decoys, made as subjects of litigation as early as 1280 and again in 1415 and 1432, referred to the tunnel nets and cages into which fowl were driven.

John Ray, writing in 1678 and describing the activities of the fenland fowlers noted "a new artifice but lately introduced from the Dutch, for the enticement of Wildfowl". There is much support for the view that duck decoys are of Dutch origin. The name itself is certainly Dutch — Eend, duck (Mallard are Wilde Eend) and Kooi, a cage or trap, Eend-kooi. The word has now gained in its shortened form, decoy, a much wider usage in the English language, and for that reason in its specific and original meaning is usually prefaced by the word "duck", which is really redundant. The Dutch shorten the word even more and refer only to kooi and British decoymen, too, invariably use the shortened version, coy.

The earliest decoy of which there is a reliable description with full particulars and cost of materials used in its construction is that made for King Charles II in St. James' Park by a Dutchman, one Sydrach Hilcus, who was imported from Holland for this specific purpose. The Royal Decoyman was, however, an Englishman named Storey, who used to enter the decoy through a gate which still bears his name.

The earliest reference to Borough Fen Decoy that has been found is an application, made in 1670, for permission to pierce the bank of the Welland in order to lead water into the decoy pond. This suggests that the decoy had at the time of the application been in use for some time and was now, as the result of an increasingly effective land drainage, drying out. It is, however, unlikely that the decoy was made before 1650, the year in which the Adventurers completed the high bank on the east side of the Welland and the course and outfall of the river been straightened, for until then the North Level and Borough Fen were still insecure against inundation.

By the turn of the 18th century there were a large number of decoys established in the fens. Defoe, writing in 1724 of North

Cambridgeshire, recorded "In these fenns are an abundance of those admirable pieces of art called Duckoys; that is to say, places so adapted for the harbour and shelter of Wildfowl, and then furnished with a breed of those so-called decoy-ducks, who are taught to allure and entice their kind to the place they belong to,

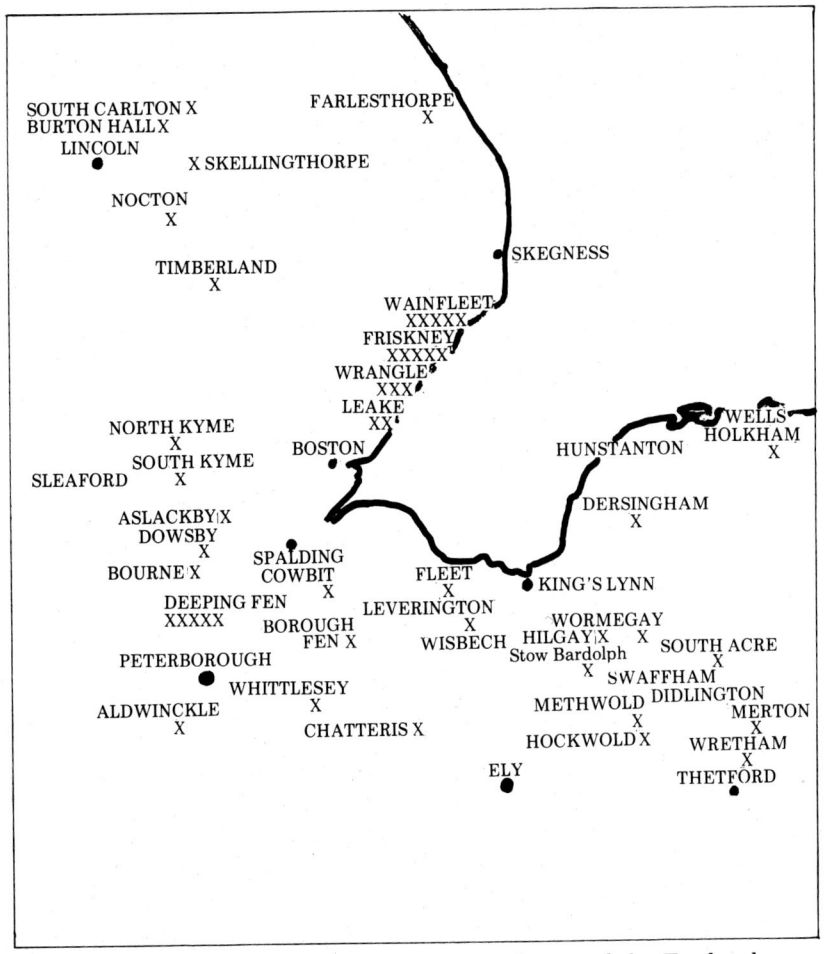

Some of the known Duck Decoys in and around the Fenland.
The cross against the name of each parish show the number of decoys in that parish. *[Payne-Gallewey]*

that it is incredible what quantities of wild-fowl of all sorts they take in these duckoys every week during the season''. After describing a decoy near Ely "which pays to the landlord, Sir. Tho. Hare, 500L a year rent, beside the charge of maintaining a great number of servants for the management'', he writes, ''There are more of these about Peterborough who send their fowl up twice a week in waggon loads at a time, whose waggons, before the last Act of Parliament to regulate carriers, I have seen drawn by ten or twelve horses apiece, they were loaded so heavy''.

Profitable as the working of a decoy was in those days, it is unlikely that the catch ever reached a weight sufficient to test the strength and endurance of ten or twelve horses and in very few seasons could the decoyman afford to pay a rent of five hundred pounds, besides his other expenses, for we have records of the prices that ducks made at that time. It is, however, certain that decoying was for a time an exceedingly profitable undertaking, for decoys sprang up in most counties in England and parts of Ireland. Payne-Gallwey was able to find records of over 200 in England and of 22 in Ireland. Not all of these were used commercially; a number were small ponds in large estates catching ducks for the table as their owners required.

This era of prosperity was short-lived. The effects of an increasingly effective drainage were more and more felt and by the beginning of the 19th century many decoys had fallen into disuse. There was increasing disturbance from an increasing population and altered land use. By 1808 over 200,000 acres had been recovered from the fenland in Lincolnshire and was under cultivation. The gradual disappearance of open water and wetlands, the essential habitat of waterfowl, had led to a reduction in the number of ducks and so long as the same number of decoys sought to get a livelihood from from the reduced number of birds, the state of affairs must have worsened.

In 1815, under the date Nov. 15th, Colonel Peter Hawker, the famous wildfowler, complaining of the shortage of ducks, wrote ''walked nearly thirty miles in surveying the Fens, and could soon perceive that they would not answer for wildfowl shooting; if a frost, the birds are gone; if a thaw, the greater part of them remain in the Decoys''. In Lincolnshire, drainage of the East and West Fens, formerly noted for the prodigious number of wildfowl in them, had been completed in 1814, a year previous to Colonel Hawker's visit. The effect appears to have been immediate. The price obtained for ducks remained exceptionally high, for it was the time of the Napoleonic Wars and the blockade, but the catches were too small for the decoys to pay their way. Fourteen years later, in 1829, Oldfield in his History of Wainfleet wrote, ''Great as are the advantages arising from the inclosure and drainage, they have in some measure been counterbalanced, as it represents this parish, by the loss sustained by the Decoys and the almost total failure of the Cranberry Harvest. Friskney was at one time noted for the number and magnitude of its Decoys, and for the immense quantity of Wildfowl caught in them. London was at that period principally supplied with Ducks, Wigeon and Teal from the Decoys in this neighbourhood. In one season, a few winters prior to the inclosure of the Fen, ten Decoys, five of which were in this parish, furnished the astonishing number of 31,200 ducks for the markets of the Metropolis. Since the inclosure the number caught has been comparatively small. Only three Decoys remain, two in Friskney, one in Wainfleet St. Mary's, and the Decoymen consider 5,000 birds as a good season''.

The decline continued. Payne-Gallwey in 1886 was only able to find forty-four still in use out of the two hundred and more he had found to be at one time in existence. In 1918 Mr J. Whitaker in his book *British Duck Decoys of Today* found only nineteen still in use. In February 1925, Herbert Williams at Borough Fen, the only member of that great family of decoymen still engaged in the traditional family occupation, received a letter from the last of that other great family of decoymen, the Skeltons, a family probably more famous than the William's because of the many mentions in Payne-Gallwey's book, a family which after leaving their no longer profitable decoys in Wainfleet and Friskney in Lincolnshire, had introduced into Norfolk and other counties the Dutch type of decoy with its small pond and demonstrated its great superiority over the large meres generally used in those parts. He wrote to say that his employer, Lord Plymouth, was closing his decoy at Orwell Park in Shropshire and that by the summer he would be without a job. He asked Herbert Williams to let him know if he heard of another.

There was no work for another decoyman. By 1936 eight more, including Orwell Park, had fallen into disuse and of the remainder only five were in regular use commercially, but the fifth at Orielton, Pembrokeshire, showed a significant change of use and had become a ringing station. In 1947 the Wildfowl Trust refurbished the Berkeley Old Decoy at Slimbridge and it too became a ringing station, and at Borough Fen Billy Williams was compensated at market prices for the Wigeon, Pintail and Teal he caught ringed and released from 1947 on. At first funds were insufficient to pay for the more expensive Mallard that he caught. After 1954 all birds were paid for and Billy was put on a salary. In 1968, the Wildfowl Trust acquired Nacton Decoy (Suffolk) on lease from the Orwell Park Estate. The records, to which the Trust was given full access, show that this was a most successful decoy whose catches have been rarely surpassed by any decoy since the 18th century. Thus the last of the commercial decoys to make a profit for its owners now makes its contributions to the conservation rather than the destruction of waterfowl.

The final chapter in the history of British duck decoys had, in fact, been written in 1952, when, under the Wild Birds Protection Act, it became illegal to catch birds for market. Permission might be given to a man who had a decoy and was still working it commercially to continue to do so, but on that man's death or retirement no licence would be issued to a successor for further commercial use.

3. Borough Fen Decoy

Borough Fen Decoy is just over 17 acres in area. It consists of 14½ acres of woodland with many intersecting paths and a pond of 2½ acres. A high boundary wire-netting fence overhangs a perimeter ditch. It was put up in 1958 to keep out foxes and rabbits and although it has been sunk well into the ground an occasional rabbit still gets in (and breeds) and, more rarely, a fox. It has, however, been successful in keeping out human intruders.

The pond would appear to some to be small in view of the number of birds it is expected or hoped to hold, but the old decoyman who knew what they were about purposely kept the pond small. A large lake or mere might hold more birds but they were likely to be out in the middle far away from any possibility of enticement into a pipe. It was the number of birds that could be caught, not the number on the pond, that mattered. The pond is shallow. When full, its depth which can be controlled by sluices is on average 15 inches and is nowhere greater than 2 feet. This again is deliberate. A shallow pond is much more attractive to the surface feeding ducks, the "dabbling ducks" such as Mallard, Pintail, Wigeon and Teal; these were the birds that made the most money at market and a decoy was essentially a commercial concern. A deeper pond would have attracted more diving ducks, Pochard and Tufted Duck, but they are almost impossible to catch in a pipe - they tend to dive and to swim back under water past the decoyman into the pond - and they are not so valuable in the market. The shallowness of the pond does, however, involve the constant invasion of the open water by reed [Phragmites communis] and its control involves the decoyman in a lot of trouble and expense. The pond is essentially a daytime roost for ducks until they fly out in the evening to feed in the nearby fields. If there were large reed beds the ducks would skulk in them and be more difficult to catch.

Except near the openings of the pipes the banks of the pond are kept steep or fenced with willow and osier cuttings and do not tempt the ducks to come ashore. Near the pipes, however, and within the pipes themselves the banks, sheltered by the "back wall" are kept mown and slope gently down to the water's edge, forming the "landings". Here the ducks sit sleeping, preening and basking in the sun, while half-in, half-out of the water others, the "loafers", stand, drift or swim purposelessly around. Such birds are all within the area of enticement into a pipe.

Within or near the entrance of the pipes are moored "wing poles", some 10 to 20 feet long, composed of narrow trunks of trees floating on the water on which ducks, especially Teal, are fond of sitting.

The pipes are dykes or channels continuous with the pond which taper from 20 feet in width at their entrance to 2 feet at the narrow end. They have a roof formed by netting stretched over hoops and the screens on one side and the back wall on the other form the sides. In Borough Fen Decoy there are eight pipes, more than in most old decoys and probably more than one would wish. The advantage of such a number lies in the fact that in any wind one, and sometimes two pipes, can be used. The disadvantage lies in the extra trouble and expense entailed in the maintenance of an unnecessary pipe, an important economic factor. The pipes are named according to the compass point at which they leave the pond - the North, the North-east, the East and so on. The North-west is called the House pipe because it is near the boat house and the farm house where the decoyman lived.

The pipes radiate from the pond like the tentacles of an octopus but no two pipes are exactly alike. This is because the pond does not lie in the middle of the wood but off-centre to the south-west, the little ends of the South, South-west and West pipes being only a short distance away from the perimeter fences whereas the North pipe ends a hundred yards from the outer margin of the wood. Close inspection suggests that the pond was originally square with a pipe arising from each corner and four others, possibly added later, from each flat side in between. After running a straight course for a varying distance the pipes curve clockwise at an angle of at least 45 degrees so that the South-east pipe at its narrow end points just to the west of south and the South pipe points to the south-west. This curve enables the decoyman to extract ducks from the tunnel net out of sight of birds on the pond, for he is screened by the vegetation on the "points", the promontories between the pipe entrances. The pipes vary in length from 180 feet at the south-west to 150 feet at the shortest pipe, the East.

A decoy pipe might be described as a funnel, consisting as it does of a system of hoops decreasing in size as they span a narrow, curving channel of water. The hoops are joined by longitudinal stringers; a net made of sisal or man-made fibres is laced over the first hoop and then stretched over the parallel stringers. A single cord is tied to each hoop about 3 feet from the base on each side of the water for the full extent of the screens. The net is then attached to this cord. This leaves a gap between the bank or landing and the net edge, which enables mowing and maintenance work to be carried out. Ducks do not attempt to escape through this gap as the screens appear to them to make with the net a continuous wall.

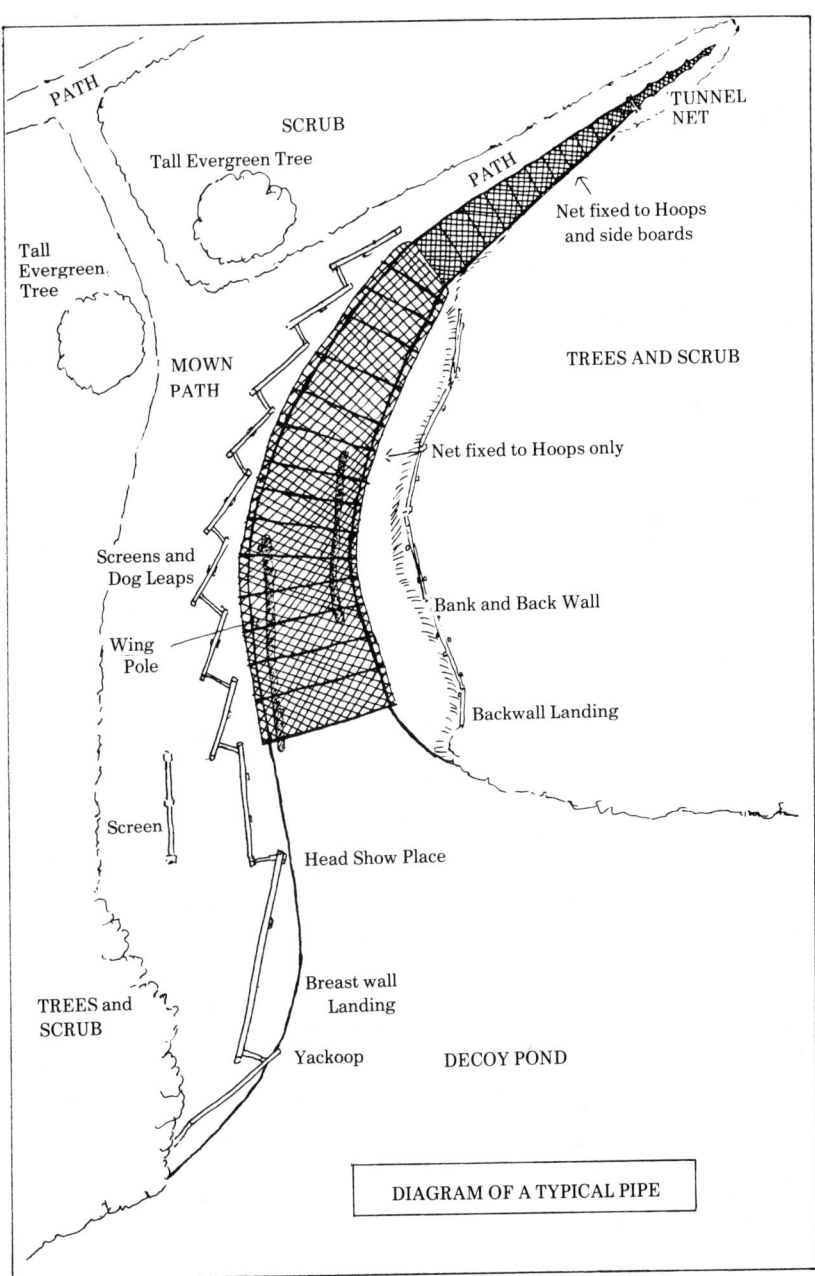

PATH

SCRUB

Tall Evergreen Tree

PATH

TUNNEL
NET

Net fixed to Hoops
and side boards

Tall
Evergreen
Tree

MOWN
PATH

TREES AND SCRUB

Net fixed to Hoops only

Screens and
Dog Leaps

Bank and Back Wall

Wing
Pole

Backwall Landing

Screen

Head Show Place

Breast wall
Landing

TREES and
SCRUB

Yackoop

DECOY POND

DIAGRAM OF A TYPICAL PIPE

The height of the first hoop from the water varies. The highest, the South-east, is 12 feet above water level. The lowest is 10 feet. The narrow or little ends, to which the hoops gradually taper and the tunnel nets are attached, are a constant 2 feet because the tunnel nets are all 2 feet in diameter and it is important that tunnel nets should be interchangeable.

Before 1958 the hoops of the eight pipes were made of wood cut from the osiers growing near the pipes that made good straight poles up to 15 feet in length. The poles were pointed at one end and then driven into the banks of the pipe, one on each side. The two free ends were then pulled together until they overlapped by 2 or 3 feet and then lashed together. With care, patience and no little skill a perfectly symmetrical curve could be produced. Unfortunately in some years a heavy snowfall would collect on the net and, in spite of the efforts of the decoyman in bitterly cold weather before dawn and the return of the ducks to dislodge it, the snow would partly thaw and impact and then when another snow-storm arrived the whole structure would collapse under the weight. In 1954 all eight pipes were completely renovated but a very heavy snowfall the following January crushed every pipe and a tangle of hoops and netting froze into the water below. In the summer of 1955 much time and money were spent in rebuilding completely all the pipes and new netting was fitted. On the 4th January the following year, a heavy fall of snow destroyed every pipe for the second consecutive year. The pipes were again completely rebuilt or, where possible, propped up. In the following summer it was decided to depart from the tradition of wooden hoops and to use metal. The first all-metal pipe was completed in 1958, since when every pipe has been modernised with metal hoops embedded in concrete on the bank, the first outer hoop being guyed with 12 gauge wire to an angle iron driven deeply into the bank. The osier lateral runners have been replaced by wire and the net, formerly of sisal, is now of man-made fibres which should give a much longer life.

On the outer side of the curve of the pipe there is a system of screens, each screen 6 feet high and 12 to 15 feet in length and overlapping its neighbour by some 8 to 10 inches. The screens are built by digging in three or four uprights to which six cross-members are added, three on each side. Common reed is then packed between the horizontal cross-members, making a traditional and very effective screen. The final effect is that of a Venetian blind laid half-open on its side, on the outer side of which the decoyman remains hidden from the ducks in the pipe near the pond but clearly visible to those further in the pipe.

The screens continue along the outer side of the curve a short distance beyond the point where the netting, gradually nearing the

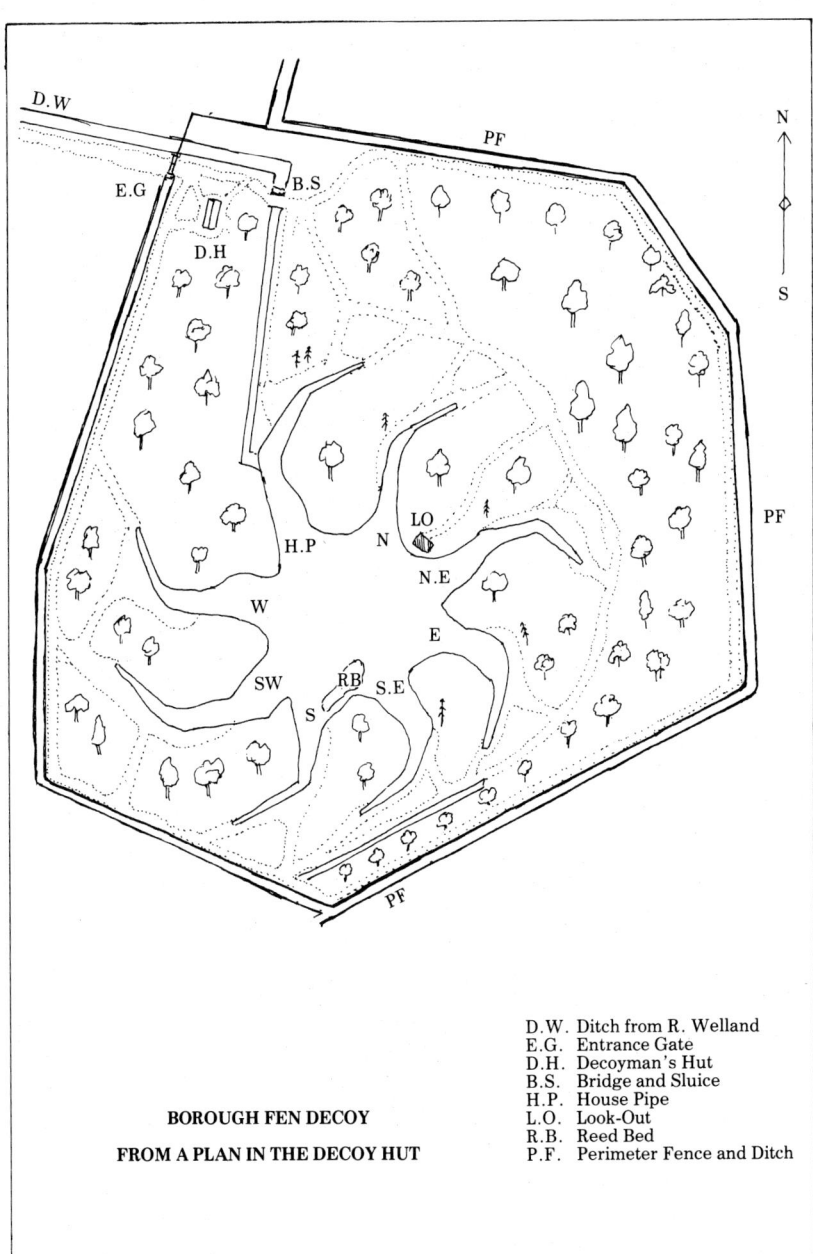

D.W. Ditch from R. Welland
E.G. Entrance Gate
D.H. Decoyman's Hut
B.S. Bridge and Sluice
H.P. House Pipe
L.O. Look-Out
R.B. Reed Bed
P.F. Perimeter Fence and Ditch

BOROUGH FEN DECOY

FROM A PLAN IN THE DECOY HUT

ground on the tapering hoops, is attached to boards on either side of the now narrow channel and completely closes it in. At the other end, the pond end, the screen is continued beyond the first hoop to what is called the Head Show Place and beyond this to the breast wall and breast wall landings with its Show Place and the delightful name of "Yackoop", believed to be a corruption of "wake-up", applicable when the birds asleep on the landings are suddenly roused.

Between the ends of each screen is a low baffle known as the "Dog Leap". This is 3 feet wide and about 18 inches high. The dog jumps from behind the screens over one of these to become suddenly visible to the ducks in the pipe and then back over another to be lost to them. The purpose of the screens and the dog leaps is explained in the next chapter.

On the inner side of the curve of the pipe there is a continuous low backwall, usually starting on the pond side of the first hoop as a backing to the landings and continuing to a point just beyond where the screens on the other side finish. At the inner narrow end of the pipe the water in the channel ends just short of the point where the side boards begin and the net is fixed. The ground slopes upwards to two stakes within which the first ring of the tunnel net is fixed. The net is pulled out its full length, about 15 feet, its far end fixed to a vertical stake and so kept on the stretch. It is detached by pulling the first hoop from between the two stakes and closed, when the ducks have run into it, by giving it a twist between hoops.

Various paths are constructed in relation to each pipe and carefully maintained by regular mowing to allow a silent approach and swift, unobstructed working.

The purpose of the woodland is to screen the pond and pipes from the outside world, not only keeping them out of sight but also doing much to deaden the noise when machinery is being used in the nearby fields and the potatoes or sugar beet are being taken up. It helps to give the ducks a sense of security so that they are more likely to come to the landings to sleep and preen rather than to keep to the centre of the pond beyond the range of enticement. The trees should not, however, be too tall, making it difficult for ducks flying near it to see the pond from the air. There should also be clear sky at the end of each pipe for ducks in their effort to escape up a pipe would be unwilling to fly into a dense canopy of trees. Trees, too, are not immortal and if as the result of old age, disease or uprooting in a gale, a large one falls across a pipe, it can do very great damage and be expensive to remove. In 1958 171 trees, mostly poplar and ash, were removed, many of which were hollow much of the distance up the trunks and in great danger of falling. It was very noticeable how the more important bushes and undergrowth improved when

24

The inside of a pipe showing wing-poles

Showing overlap of screens

Showing how the overlap of screens gives the appearance of a continuous wall

Piper taking a dog-leap as he comes out of a pipe after being shown to the ducks

Ducks view of little end of pipe
[photo: Anne Treadwell-Cook]

Looking out of south-west pipe. Note lookout and entrance to north-east pipe
[photo: Anne Treadwell-Cook]

Piper at work with Tony Cook observing through the reed screen
[photo: Anne Treadwell-Cook].

Tony Cook breaking the ice
[photo: Anne Treadwell-Cook]

Feeding the pipe
[photo: Anne Treadwell-Cook]

Ring on Mallard's foot
[photo: Anne Treadwell-Cook]

Piper watches as a ring is attached
[photo: Anne Treadwell-Cook]

Billy Williams repairing the traditional type of pipe made of osier poles grown in the Decoy wood, and sisal netting.

Billy Williams with his two dogs, Nella and Amber, asleep in the sun. He is resting against the oak tree brought by Tom Williams (1770-1870) as a seedling from Lakenheath Decoy about the year 1810, and planted just outside Borough Fen Decoy gates

Billy Williams standing by the portrait of his great-great-grandfather, John Williams (1741-1825). A portrait of the horse of Joseph Williams (1793-1871), Billy's great-great-uncle, hangs beside it.

Aerial view of Borough Fen Decoy 1981

the dense cover of the large trees had been removed.

Formerly the osiers, regularly pollarded, and the hazels coppiced down to ground level, provided material for the making and mending of pipes and screens and also of baskets in which the ducks were sent to market, and eel traps, an additional source of income for the decoymen.

4. The Technique of Catching Ducks, as Practiced in Borough Fen Decoy

Three basic techniques are used in Borough Fen Decoy for the purpose of catching ducks - baiting the pipes, flushing birds from the landings and wing poles, and, the most exciting method, luring the ducks into the pipe by means of a dog.

The method used on any one occasion will depend on a number of factors of which the weather generally and particularly the force and direction of the wind, the time of day and the length of shadows, and the lethargy or awareness of the ducks are the most important.

The first consideration will be the direction of the wind for this determines which of the eight pipes can be used, since waterfowl are reluctant to take off tail to wind. Usually two pipes can be used, the ideal one being that where the wind is blowing diagonally from the tunnel net. For example, the South-east pipe is most successfully operated with a south-westerly wind. Then the wind is blowing towards the ducks facing into the pipe but it carries away from the pond any human scent or sound of movement. The South pipe may also be used in a wind from the south-west, but then the decoyman must be particularly careful as any scent or sound will then be blown parallel to the screens and with a slight eddy or change in wind direction will be wafted over the water and alert the ducks.

Although it varies in its degree of success from year to year baiting is the most productive of the three techniques. In the 1959/60 season, out of 3,312 ducks caught 2,204 were taken by baiting whereas in 1961/62, from a total of 2,534, 1,180 were caught by the same means.

Food is placed in the pipes from late July to early March and since the prevailing winds are south-westerly the South-east, South and West pipes are fed the most heavily. Then, if as commonly happens, the wind changes later in the day and veers to the north-west, it may be possible to catch in the morning in the South-east pipe and at dusk in the West.

Grain weed seed and, when available, frozen potatoes are placed on the banks and in the shallow water inside the pipe but not outside the first screen. This is done at late dusk or at night after the ducks have left the pond on their evening flight to the fields. This evening flight can be a most impressive sight, especially in September when there may be as many as 1,500 ducks using the pond as a daytime roost. It is usually closely watched for it is the most reliable way for the decoyman to assess the number of ducks on the pond, many of which will have spent the day out of sight, sleeping or skulking among the reeds.

Usually the decoyman goes to the look-out hut on the point between the North and North-east pipes from where he can get a good view into the mouths of most of the pipes. If he finds that all has gone to plan and that, although some of the poorer feed has floated across the pond, the ducks are feeding on the better grain which has sunk to the bottom within the pipe, he creeps to the furthest screen at the show place of that pipe, where he is in full view of the birds actually in the pipe but still hidden from those on the pond. The ducks in the pipe immediately panic and fly in confusion down the narrowing tunnel, some without stopping, into the tunnel net, while others alight on the water and half-flying, half-swimming, are driven onwards before the decoyman who walks swiftly from screen to screen, continually visible to the ducks in the pipe but always hidden from those on the pond. All the ducks dash to the far end of the tunnel net where they bunch huddled together. The tunnel net is held in position close against the last hoop of the pipe and the side boards by two short vertical stakes. When all the catch is in the far end the first hoop is lifted up from its anchored position, the first segment is given a twist and the catch is now complete.

All this sounds very straightforward and simple but unfortunately there are a number of things that may, and very commonly do, go wrong. After feeding two or three pipes the wind may change overnight and the ducks, no longer catchable, may get a banquet in safety. Often the smaller birds in the decoy, the sparrows and finches, feed on the grain on the bank margin, while others, waiting to feed or already fed, perch on the net above. It is impossible for the decoymen to approach without being seen by birds on the top of the net and they fly off warning their fellows on the ground and the ducks on the water who swim quietly out onto the pond. The decoyman "shows" to an empty pipe where moments before the quarry had been contentedly feeding.

When the ducks arrive back in the morning after a night gleaning in the fields they usually have a wash and a preen and then sleep through the morning. As afternoon passes they begin to wake up and to feel hungry and look round for a meal. This late afternoon movement into baited pipes, a time when feeding a pipe is most likely to bring results, coincides with the appearance of roosting pheasants and pigeons. Again, as the decoyman silently picks his show place, these sharp-eyed creatures crash noisily from the trees and undergrowth, spreading alarm through what were potentially catchable ducks.

The second method is the flushing of birds from prepared sites by showing at the show place. After their return to the decoy in the morning although they are content enough after a wash and a preen to spend the day sleeping on the water, the ducks will tend to drift wherever a breeze may take them and they have to wake at intervals to correct their position or avoid a collision with a resentful duck. Warm, sheltered places have, however, been prepared for them on the landings in the pipes and at their entrances where the mown banks slope gently down to the water's edge. Here and on the wing poles the ducks congregate. The pipes most attractive to these sleepers and loafers are the North-west, the North and the North-east which catch the best of the sun from nine in the morning to three o'clock in the afternoon. Unfortunately there is little shelter from the prevailing south-west wind and this situation cannot be exploited as often as one would wish.

Ducks appear to sleep with one eye open and are alert at the slightest sound. The cry of a waterhen or the faint sound of the decoyman's footstep, although the last 20 feet or so of the path may be covered in sawdust to soften the sound, will destroy that essential element of surprise which will turn to panic, when he arrives at the show place.

The third and most exciting method and the most skilful is by the use of a dog. It is always said that the dog, traditionally called "Piper", should resemble a fox but be slightly smaller. He should be ginger or yellow in colour with a bushy or curly conspicuous tail.

The present "Piper" has many of these characters but they are not essential. Herbert Williams used a small black mongrel and white wire-haired terriers; Billy used a white terrier with a large spot on its back and later two yellow labradors, Nella and Amber, while at Fritton Decoy they used for a number of years with every success a large Newfoundland-type of dog.

The temperament and natural behaviour of a dog, and, above all, its training are probably far more important than its appearance. A decoy dog must be completely obedient responding to a single movement of its master's hand, always taking the dog-leap its master indicates, running smartly in front of the screens without stopping for an instant, without a whine or a whimper, never turning to face the ducks, disappearing quickly over the next dog-leap to return and sit in silence at its master's feet. But even when a well-trained dog of perfect colour and appearance is used, ducks appear to go "stale", particularly towards the end of the season, and to take no notice of the dog. Sometimes a change of dog or a change in the dog's appearance will have an effect. A coloured cloth tied to Spot's collar appeared to reawaken the duck's interest but the dog did not seem to work as well and appeared to resent being dressed up.

Young ducks respond to the dog more readily than older ones but as the season advances all ages show a much weakened response. Although some birds have been caught as many as seven times in their lifetime and some even three times on one day, the majority seem to remember their experience and after their release are reluctant to follow the dog and enter the pipe a second time. The hesitancy of these experienced birds appears to affect the other inexperienced birds.

Other animals besides dogs have been frequently used. Billy Williams for a time used a cat, to which (when it behaved properly, which was not very often) the ducks responded well but it was not amenable to discipline and impossible to control. A stuffed fox and a stuffed stoat have both been used at Borough Fen, the former being presented to the ducks from behind successive screens, the latter being made to appear to run from screen to screen along the top. The ducks responded and some were caught by these artifices. The method was, however, more useful as a means of investigating the reaction of ducks to the sudden appearance of a known predator rather than as a means of catching ducks. The method, too, had none of the versatility of command of a dog.

There has always been considerable controversy as to why ducks do follow the decoyman's dog. It would appear to be a mixture of curiosity, the ducks never being allowed a good look at a strange object - hence the value of a smartly moving dog disappearing as suddenly as it came - and of aggression, the mobbing instinct, the attack on a known or suspected predator, as when cows follow a strange dog in a field, and small birds mob a hawk or an owl in daylight.

Sir Ralph Payne-Gallwey gives instances which may not be helpful in the elucidation of the reason for this pursuit reaction, but which are so amusing that they more than justify inclusion here although they did not occur in Borough Fen. "I have tried a cat, a ferret and a rabbit", he writes in *The Book of Duck Decoys*. "They all attract but are next to impossible to manage. I once bribed an organ-grinder to lend me his monkey. The fowl absolutely flew after him when first shown, but when he turned round and grinned at them they fled. When he sprang atop a screen and cracked the nuts I had tried to bribe him with into acquiescence, ending by scampering along the top of the pipe, every bird left the Decoy for the day. And no wonder. Finally the monkey tumbled in the Decoy and nearly died from fright and cold and I narrowly missed having to replace him".

Whatever the cause may be, ducks do under certain conditions react to the sudden appearance of a dog by following it, and the fullest advantage may be taken of this reaction by training a dog to bring about these conditions. The system of screens and dog-leaps is designed to allow the dog to be visible to the birds for just a few seconds and then to disappear as suddenly as it appeared.

The procedure when working the dog is as follows. Having tested the wind and, possibly, having seen from the look-out ducks near the entrance of a pipe or actually in it, the decoyman walks silently along the path to the pipe, selects a suitable screen through which, by parting the reeds with a sliver of wood, he can determine the exact position of the ducks. If they prove to be actually in the pipe there will be no need to show the dog and by going to the show place he can drive the ducks along into the tunnel net. If, however, the ducks are mostly outside the first hoop, he will put the dog over a dog-leap one or two screens away from them. He may continue to show the dog two or three times. He parts again the reeds in a screen to see where the ducks are and how they are reacting. If he has been successful and the ducks are entering the pipe he continues to send the dog over the dog-leaps one or more screen ahead of them while he follows screen by screen. As long as the ducks can see the dog, they continue to pursue it. When the dog disappears, they stop and swim about, their necks outstretched, trying to see where he has gone. The dog suddenly reappears, there is a reawakening of excitement and the pursuit is resumed. When he judges the ducks are sufficiently far in the pipe and he has a worthwhile catch, the decoyman signals to his dog to ''sit'' while he suddenly appears at the show place and, reinforcing his movements by waving a piece of cloth or his handkerchief, he runs along the outer side of the screens, driving the ducks before him, taking great care not to disturb the ducks behind him on the pond. If the ducks are well in the pipe there is no need to go as far as the head of the pipe, but he may show at any place, so long as it is behind the ducks, who will be facing away from him and still searching for the dog.

Sometimes, apart from when they have become "stale", ducks do not follow the dog readily. Somehow their mood or the conditions are not quite right; often they will come to the mouth of the pipe but refuse to be drawn right in. On other occasions two or three will swim into the pipe while the greater number stay outside. On such occasions the dog can be taken back level with them and its sudden appearance, almost on top of them, will so reinforce their response after their surprise that they will follow eagerly.

"Dogging" brings its own problems. It is necessary to work close to the screens and therefore close to the pond. Long shadows in the autumn and winter restrict certain pipes to early morning and evening use. For example, the West pipe cannot be used on a sunny day between 10 a.m. and noon as the sun throws a shadow across the dog-leaps. Great care, too, must be taken when looking along the sliver of wood for, should the sun be on one's back, a break in the screen would allow a shaft of light to fall across the water and alarm the ducks.

There must be no sound whatever other than the slight noise of movement the ducks can attribute to the dog, and extraneous noises will often prevent the ducks coming up the pipes. The type of crop growing in the fields round the decoy may influence the catch. If the fields on the south and west sides are growing cereals there is some disturbance whilst these are being harvested in August and September. If on the other hand potatoes or sugar beet are being grown, these will be harvested and the disturbance is in October and November. In a fine dry autumn, harvesting may be complete in a few days. If the weather is very wet, the operation may go on intermittently for several weeks.

Neither Herbert nor Billy Williams had much use for "call ducks". They both considered that they could spoil the chance of a good catch and that they were generally more trouble than they were worth. There is no evidence that they were ever used to any extent in Borough Fen Decoy.

Call ducks appear originally to have been white, so that the decoyman could recognise his own birds even in the dark; smaller, because small birds were thought to eat less than large ones, and to be noisier than normal birds so that they were likely to "call" the wild birds in. They were trained to feed well up a pipe and to take no notice of the decoyman and his dog, with whom, being hand-reared, they were perfectly familiar. The wild birds, seeing the call ducks feeding, would follow into the pipe.

The call ducks were fed in the late evening after the wild birds had left. If they were too well fed (and had eaten most of the feed left in the pipes for the wild birds) they came poorly or not at all in the daytime and enticed no wild birds in. If they were under-fed, they dashed across the pipe when the food was presented to them to the alarm of the wild birds on the pond. The breed became noisy and aggressive and destroyed the peace and quiet of the pond. It was thought that hand-reared wild ducks might be useful but they were rather worse. They hung about the entrance of the pipes and attacked the true wild birds and prevented them entering.

It was found difficult to feed the pipes in the daytime, when the call ducks in spite of a reasonably good evening meal would still come in and feed. However carefully it was thrown in, the patter of the grain, as it fell on the water, made the wild birds suspicious if not actually alarmed. Call ducks have, however, been used with great success at other decoys.

The only time that call ducks are certainly of value is at the beginning of the season. After many weeks of disturbance during the summer when repair work has been carried out and the pond has partially or completely dried out, there are no ducks left. If a nucleus of call ducks is kept, they will certainly speed up the lead in and build up a strong roosting population.

Another way of increasing the duck population on the pond, seldom used at Borough Fen, is known as "raising the pond". When there are only a few ducks on the pond and yet there still appears to be a large local population in the district, when a large number of ducks are seen to be flying over, the ducks on the pond are deliberately flushed. They fly up and join the large number overhead and knowing they are well fed and cared for they will soon fly back, bringing (it is hoped) the larger number with them. This can be a risky business and it is not unknown for the small number to be lost as well.

Whatever the method used, the art of decoying lies basically in getting the ducks so far up the pipe that the decoyman, without disturbing the birds on the pond, can get between them and their way of escape.

5. Ringing and Recoveries

Until 1947 the decoy was operated purely as a commercial entity, but by then the market price of edible waterfowl was lagging behind the general cost of living. The meat ration which had been minute during the war had increased and was finally phased out in 1952 and the demand for waterfowl was much reduced. The Wildfowl Enquiry Committee offered to pay the market price for each duck ringed and released and this arrangement continued until 1951, when the decoy was taken over by the Wildfowl Trust. For the first six years only species other than Mallard were ringed because they had a lower market value and formed a smaller percentage of the catch. In 1954 the scheme was extended to include all species and since that year no ducks caught at Borough Fen Decoy have been killed for food. Later the decoyman was paid a salary rather than on the basis of each duck caught as his duties now included general conservation and ringing operations in the area, the care of static traps at the Deeping St. James ballast pits, and wader and goose counts on the Wash.

From 1947 to 1977, 40,716 ducks were ringed at Borough Fen. Annual totals fluctuated widely from a record 3,150 in 1967 down to 350 in 1955. Mallard predominated with Teal a good second. Species caught were Mallard 29,795; Teal 10,516; Pintail 72; Shoveler 253; Wigeon 67; Gadwall 4; Garganey 9.

Table 1 Showing the Number of Ducks Taken in Each
Pipe in a Good Year (1959/60) and a Moderate Year (1960/61)

1959/60

Month	House	N.	NE.	E.	Pipe SE.	S.	SW.	W.	Total.
July								2	2
August			6	43	125	37	7	112	330
Sept.	31		22	146	411	214	3	302	1129
Oct.				79	257	126	40	171	673
Nov.				37	163	99	60	161	520
Dec.			2	42	108	4	77	82	315
Jan.				31	81	10	15	71	208
Feb.	5			7	33	28	4	31	108
March.	1			6	10	2	1	7	27
Total	37	0	30	391	1188	520	207	937	3312

1960/61

Month	House	N.	NE.	E.	Pipe SE.	S.	SW.	W.	Total
July	1				4			5	10
August		5		11	49			79	144
Sept		64		92	139	132		164	591
Oct.		30		38	85	60		95	308
Nov.		11		6	34	9		20	78
Dec.					12	18		14	44
Jan.				3	37	20		27	87
Feb.				2	28	4		12	46
March				2	5	2			9
Total	1	110	0	154	393	245	0	416	1319

A detailed analysis of Mallard recoveries was made by Ogilvie and Cook in 1971 and 1972, divided into two parts, those ringed at the decoy and recovered abroad, and those recovered in the British Isles. The analysis of the British recoveries was made from 23,968 ringed in the twelve years between the 1957/58 and the 1970/71 catching seasons and the foreign recoveries from the 17,340 ringed from 1957/58 to 1966/67.

Boyd and Ogilvie (1961) showed that Mallard ringed in the decoy wandered little during the winter of ringing, 22% of recoveries being within ten miles and 90% being within an irregular boundary varying between 40 and 80 miles from the decoy and largely following watersheds. A further important finding was that no less than 86% of recoveries in the season after ringing were in this "dispersion area", further indicating the sedentariness of British-bred Mallard and the adoption of traditional winter areas by immigrant Mallard from the Continent. By the end of their first season 47.5% of Mallard ringed at Borough Fen have been shot and at the end of the fourth season 88% are dead. Practically none are left alive at the end of ten years although there is one outstanding

34

recovery of a female Mallard ringed in 1955 and reported shot at Thurlby seven miles to the north in 1975, twenty years after ringing. An even older male Mallard ringed in October 1957 was shot six miles away at Crowland in September 1978.

Table II Showing the Number of Ducks Taken in Each of the Months of the Season of Two Typical Years by Three Methods Described Above.

Month	Piper (Dog)		Feeding		Bank and Wing Poles		Total	
	59/60	61/62	59/60	61/62	59/60	61/62	59/60	61/62
April-July			2	12	2			12
August	187	436	6	53	137	53	330	542
Sept.	480	381	629	150	20	78	1129	609
Oct.	141	161	532	234		13	673	407
Nov.	56	119	461	203	3		520	322
Dec.	16	18	299	119		2	315	139
Jan.	24	13	184	138			208	151
Feb.	42	42	66	132		2	108	176
March		31	27	93			27	124,
April				52				52
Total	946	1200	2204	1186	162	148	3312	2534

Mallard produce about 20% recoveries overall with 3.7% overseas, of the 17,340 analysed 659 were reported from east and north-east Europe with a handful from France and Spain. The range of these overseas recoveries has been divided into three parts:-

1. The Urals, west to Norway   244 birds
2. Poland, East and West Germany, Denmark   201 birds
3. The Netherlands, Belgium, North and Central France   214 birds

The eastermost area is the simplest to consider since all the recoveries will be of birds breeding there and not passing through. Over the ten years reviewed 54.6% of the 2,444 reported were drakes.

Table III

Numbers of Mallard ringed each month 1957/58 to 1970/71

Season	July/Aug	Sept.	Oct.	Nov	Dec.	Jan.	Feb/Mar.	Total
1957/58	5	736	102	211	190	73	91	1408
1958/59	78	592	386	341	207	63	75	1742
1959/60	322	1031	548	331	164	105	73	2574
1960/61	133	515	238	67	28	59	39	1079
1961/62	516	479	271	187	65	90	175	1783
1962/63	98	663	257	170	50	0	20	1258
1963/64	223	648	338	170	42	95	75	1591
1964/65	666	1027	454	326	22	26	75	2596
1965/66	413	523	123	17	14	25	27	1142
1966/67	481	986	237	209	108	53	113	2167
1967/68	374	1171	563	278	105	63	65	2619
1968/69	264	554	238	189	51	15	9	1320
1969/70	211	738	193	267	76	53	51	1589
1970/71	219	610	61	98	52	35	25	1100
Totals	4003	10273	3989	2861	1174	755	913	23968

35

The Mallard in Area 2 are clearly of mixed origin, some are local and some are passing through from Area 1. There is an astonishing imbalance of sexes from this area with 75% drakes, that is, 150 out of 201 birds.

The Mallard recovered from Area 3 will be of the most mixed origins and will include not only those breeding there but also others passing through from Areas 1 and 2. Again drakes predominate with 62.9%, a less dramatic figure than that from Area 2. A possible explanation of this preponderance of drakes could be that drakes moult earlier than ducks and move out over the North Sea first and are therefore available for ringing over a long period. Another possible explanation of the odd sex ratio could be that of abmigration, the pairing of birds bred in the resident population of the Fens and flying to the northern breeding grounds with the returning migrants. There is, however, no evidence that drakes do abmigrate more readily than ducks.

Breeding success of Mallard indicated by the percentage of juveniles caught at Borough Fen in July, August and September.

Season	% Juveniles	Season	% Juveniles
1959/60	93	1965/66	81
1960/61	98	1966/67	95
1961/62	90	1967/68	84
1962/63	86	1968/69	92
1963/64	99	1969/70	95
1964/65	93	1970/71	86

The 659 foreign recoveries used in the analysis show the general pattern of migration into the eastern counties of England, but some exceptional and unexpected recoveries have made the headlines. One duck Mallard, ringed in September 1962, was shot in Alberta on the Canada-United States border in December 1965. A Teal ringed on the 9th November 1952 was shot on Barrell Island, Newfoundland on the 6th December the same year, having crossed the Atlantic in the course of those twenty-eight days. Wigeon, which breed further east, have been reported as far east beyond Moscow as Borough Fen is west. The Wigeon was recovered in the Tomsk region (85° east).

The records of ringing in table III show clearly the large proportion of the annual catch taken in September. This is the period when the greater part of the population are birds hatched that year and the adults are hiding away flightless in full moult. Table IV shows the percentage of juveniles in the catch July to September.

A similar analysis of Teal ringed at Borough Fen showed that they breed further north than Mallard for there are many recoveries from within the Arctic Circle in north-west Russia. With the onset of hard weather Teal move south-west into Ireland and then on to the Camargue and Iberia. There is one recovery of a Teal from Turkey.

36

6. The Natural History of the Borough Fen Decoy

Although Borough Fen Decoy, since its foundation over three centuries ago, has remained undisturbed in that it has escaped the plough and the changes in ecology which may follow the use by modern agriculture of sprays and fertilisers, it must be remembered that it is basically an artifact, made for the express purpose of catching ducks and managed continuously over the years for that purpose. The form of management required has governed to a great extent its ecology.

The decoy pond was probably sited where some form of pond already existed but its present form with its eight pipes was obviously man-made. The osiers would be taken from the surrounding carr and the trees, providing shelter and seclusion, from the wooded higher and drier areas of the fenland. It has been suggested that the coppiced stools of some of the hazels still present in the wood may date from the decoy's earliest days. Osiers were extensively grown in the Fens for the making of baskets and eel-traps and they were certainly planted in the decoy for this purpose, especially near the pipes where they would be conveniently placed for the maintenance work.

Judging from the stumps of the trees that have been felled and those that stand today it is probable that the decoy was at least 150 years old before other than local indigenous trees were introduced. It is interesting that Tom William's oak tree from Lakenheath, planted about 1810, was placed outside the decoy wood.

Successive decoymen appear to have added trees as much for the sake of variety as for any utilitarian purpose and no regular policy of afforestation existed... Indeed, any policy would have been difficult to carry out in view of the necessity for absolute quiet in the catching season and a close season already more than fully occupied by maintenance work. There was a tendency for mature and diseased trees to accumulate. In 1958, 171 trees were cleared. Although a few of these were sound and had been felled to pay for the cost of removing the others, many were unsafe and threatening to follow the lead of a large poplar that had already fallen and completely crushed a pipe. The work of clearance took two years to complete but the benefit from the removal of these light-shielding trees and the overcrowding was very soon apparent.

About a hundred and fifty years ago the possibilities of the decoy wood as an orchard and garden appear to have been realised. Apples, pears, quinces, bullaces and others were planted together with some flowering shrubs. This "gardening" reached its height when Herbert Williams (1856—1929) took over. He delighted to give parties and to entertain his friends in the decoy in the close season and in order to make it as attractive as possible, he planted a large number of roses, lilies, daffodils, snowdrops and many flowering plants. As a result there has been brought together a varied community of plants, often in an unnatural association of indigenous and introduced species, which has produced a rich terrestrial fauna, while the aquatic fauna has remained relatively poor.

The value of the woodland as a conservation area has been enhanced in recent years by the reduction in hedgerows and the few remaining copses in the surrounding countryside. At all times the form of management has tended to produce a marginal fringe of relatively tall protective trees and, within, a denser shrub layer intersected by many paths and rides, making it particularly attractive to small birds and certain orders of insects.

The soil of Borough Fen is mainly alluvial clay and silt overlying gravel, typical of the Welland Basin. In the decoy the depth of each is variable. Patches of peat, absent from the decoy, appear in the surrounding fields and about two miles away become a continuous deposit.

PLANTS

Moss Layer. As there is a damp micro-climate within the decoy mosses are common and, although as yet little worked, would be of interest to the specialist. There is a well-marked area of pure Thamnium (Porotrichum) alopecurum Mitt. extending for about half an acre in the fringe woodland near the east and south-east pipes. Much of the rest of the ground appears to be covered by a complex association comprising Thuidium tamariscinum Bruch and Schimper, Brachythecium rutabulum B & S., Mnium undulatum L., Eurhynchium spp., Fissidens taxifolius Hedw.

Field Layer. Apart from three small areas, the greater part is covered by nettles and hemlock. Within this community there are scattered societies of Dryppteris filix-mas (L) Schott. (Male Fern), the grasses Avena sp., Calamagrostis epigejos (L), Phleum pratense L., Holcus lanatus L., and the herbs Stachys sylvatica L., Heracleum sphondylium L, Arum maculatum L and Galium aparine L but along the pipes near to the screens, Ranunculus bulbosus L., R. repens L., and Pontentilla anserina L cover most of the ground surface. Between the house-pipe and the north pipe plants include Phragmites communis Trin., Convolvulus arvensis L., Mecurialis perennis L., Lamium album L. and Rumex acetosa L.

38

Between the north-east and east pipes the main constituents of the vegetation comprise; Arrhenatherum elatius L., Dactylis glomerata L, Symphytum officinale L., Cirsium palustre Scopoli, Polygonum persicaria L., Myosotis scorpioides L., Iris pseudacorus L., Scutellaria galericulata L., Glechoma hederacea L., Stellaria spp. and Carex spp. Between the south-west and west pipes a section is quite distinct and indicated by the conspicuous grass Festuca gigantea Vill. Some of the prominent species are Geranium robertianum L., Symphtum officinale L., Stachys sylvatica L. and Geum urbanum L.

Near the house pipe and the boundary fence are many introduced species such as snowdrops, daffodils, narcissi and lilies with "wild" species such as Geranium robertianum L., Tussilago farafra L., Chelidonium majus L., Anemone nemorosa L. and Viola sp.

Tree layer.. Although dominated by Salix Spp., the woodland contains a mixture of trees, the result of several centuries of random planting. There is much Sambucus nigra L. (Elder) from young trees to complete senescence, some thick stands of Prunus spinosa L. (Blackthorn) but only poor specimens of Betula verrucosa Ehrhart. (Birch) and the conifers, Picea abies Karsten and Larix decidua Miller, planted by previous decoy men at the bend of the pipes, are in very poor condition.

ANIMALS

Fish
Four species of fishes occur in the pond. The Sticklebacks and Minnows seldom stray far from the sluice through which the filler dyke flows. Eels stray further but seldom reach any considerable size.

Amphibians
There has been over the past twenty or more years a progressive decline in the numbers of Amphibia and Reptiles in the surrounding Fenland, where they were at one time so common, and this decline has been marked within the decoy. After the exceptionally hard winter of 1962-63 all species completely disappeared. Frogs were introduced as spawn in 1968 and 1969 and forty-two as adults in 1970. Since then a few have stayed and bred but the numbers remain low. Toads, previously common, have not been seen since 1963 although eight were introduced in 1970. Smooth Newts are very common in the feeder dyke outside the decoy but are seldom seen in the pond.

Grass snakes were abundant and bred freely in the decoy twenty years ago. They have returned in small numbers and have been seen oddly in every year since 1972.

Mammals

Of the Insectivora, Hedgehogs, Moles, Common, Water and Pygmy Shrews are common within the decoy. Only five species of bats have been recorded. The Pipistrelle and Long-eared Bats are common; Noctules, which used to roost in numbers in the large hollow trees before they were cleared in 1958, are still seen not uncommonly, flying high over the decoy in the early evening and may still roost there.

Bats with their slow flight skimming close to the water of the decoy pond, present most years, are almost certainly Daubenton's Bats, although there is no record of one being identified in the hand. The presence of Natterer's Bat rests on the finding of a single specimen dead outside the decoy man's hut in September 1950.

In spite of what should be an effective perimeter fence, Rabbits still gain entry into the decoy and although apparently wiped out by myxomatosis, a colony quickly re-establishes itself in the wood and causes damage by destroying the young osier sets and making holes in the tunnel nets. Hares, however, common in the wood before the fence was put up, do appear to be effectively kept out.

Bank Voles, Short-tailed (Field) Voles and Water Voles, although varying in numbers from year to year, are generally common.

Wood (Long-tailed Field) Mice are abundant, probably because their predators, Owls and Kestrels, have suffered a marked decrease in numbers locally. A thriving colony of House Mice lived and bred for many years in an old mattress in the decoy man's hut.

The exact year in which the last Red Squirrel and the first Grey Squirrel were seen has not been recorded. The Red Squirrel has not been seen since the Second War. The Grey Squirrel appeared shortly before the war and is an irregular visitor.

Foxes used to occur commonly in the decoy before the perimeter fence was put up in 1958. They often bred there, having moved out of the wooded hunting country a few miles to the west and, crossing the railway, they settled in the first secluded woodland they encountered. They were not encouraged for, apart from the danger to the decoy man's poultry, it was felt that they disturbed the ducks on the pond and had an adverse effect on "dogging". The fence is, even now, not wholly effective and as recently as the summer of 1976 a dog fox was seen to walk across the dried-out pond.

Since the theory of catching ducks by dogging rests on the belief that ducks follow a dog either from curiosity or from the mobbing instinct, looking upon it as a predator, it is interesting to see how ducks do, in fact, behave in the presence of a known predator, the fox.

One year, in early January, a fox which had been asleep in a reed bed, was seen to walk to the ice on the edge of the pond. It tested the ice with a front paw, found that it would not bear and walked back through the reed bed to the bank. It passed within twelve yards of some Teal resting on the ice. The drakes shuffled a little on the ice, one or two raised their heads and crests and uttered their typical "primp" call, but there was no evidence of alarm and only of a short-lived interest. It was thought that they had been aware of the fox's presence for some time and that they recognised its mood which was not hunting.

On another occasion a fox was seen to walk along one of the points on the side of the pond and to lie down in the sun. It was probably grooming itself for at intervals it was seen to put its head up from amongst the grass and to look across the pond. There were only a few Mallard on the water and those nearest it, about fifteen yards away, showed an obvious interest. They swam nearer the site where they had last seen the fox, and with their necks up-stretched trod water. When the fox looked up they showed disquiet and swam a short distance away but when the fox put its head down and was no longer visible they remained restless, swimming round in small circles but not going any nearer the fox. Their behaviour was very similar to that of ducks at the mouth of a pipe "that won't come to the dog". The fox, hidden by the grass, slunk off without being seen and the ducks soon appeared to forget about the incident.

A fox was surprised by Billy Williams and ran along the edge of the pond. It had made a sudden appearance and was running towards some of the ducks, the nearer of which immediately took wing, others dashing across the water in obvious alarm. The fox disappeared into the decoy wood. On another occasion Billy disturbed a fox which ran across the ice of the frozen pond to the alarm of the ducks roosting on it. It was unable to get a sound foothold on the ice and it kept slipping and in an effort to maintain its balance it went through an astonishing acrobatic performance. Billy said that the feeling of alarm amongst the ducks appeared to change at first to that of interest and later, he liked to think, to that of amusement.

Otters used to occur commonly in the decoy when the banks of the Welland within Crowland and Cowbit Washes were tree-lined and less regularly mown. The last record is of a sighting in 1959.

Insects

A list of the Lepidoptera is given in Appendix C. The pond life is described by Palmer, Margaret. 1974. The ecology of the invertebrate community of Borough Fen Decoy Pond, Wildfowl Trust Ann. Rep. 25: 143-148.

7. The Williams Family

To write of Borough Fen Decoy is to write of the Williams family; a family engaged in working the decoy from its earliest days until the death, three centuries later, of the last of this long line of decoymen, Billy Williams. The family was associated with at least eleven other decoys in the country, but Borough Fen, the place where many learnt their art, was always the family home.

The record of the first Williams of Borough Fen was found almost by accident. John Bradley Williams, who lived at the decoy two centuries after its foundation, being an officer employed by the Commissioners of the Bedford Level, had cause in the course of his professional duties to visit the Commissioners' offices at Ely. While searching through some old documents he found in one of the minute books, dated 1670, an application by a Mr Williams on behalf of the Earl of Lincoln, requesting permission to pierce the bank of the River Welland in order to lead a ditch to his decoy pond to supply it with water. It seems probable that the decoy had then been in existence for some years, but the increasing efficiency of the drainage had led to its drying out, and a regular and controlled water supply was essential for its maintenance. Permission was granted and Mr Williams was enabled to continue to catch ducks for the Earl.

The next Williams, of whom there is record, is Andrew of Aston Hall. He was probably a younger son, who learnt his art at Borough Fen but left home to practice it. The decoy was made by Thomas Lloyd, who died in 1692, the year in which Andrew was born. Andrew went to Aston Hall in Shropshire in 1716 at the age of 24 and stayed there until his death. In Davies' *History of Whittington Castle*, wrote Sir Payne-Gallwey. ''the following very curios lines, quoted from an epitaph, occur:-

ANDREW WILLIAMS

Born A.D. 1692. Died April 18, 1776.

Aged 84 years.

Of which he lived under the Aston Family as Decoyman

60 years.

Here lies the Decoyman who lived like an otter,
Dividing his time betwixt land and water;
His hide he oft soaked in the waters of Perry,
Whilst Aston old beer his spirits kept cherry.
Amphibious his life, Death was puzzled to say
How to dust to reduce such well-moistened clay;
So Death turned Decoyman and 'coyed him to land,
Where he fixed his abode till quite dry to the hand,
He then found him fitting for crumbling to dust,
And here he lies mouldering as you and I must''.

The river, from which a tributary ran to feed the decoy pond, was called the Perry.

No certain record of the second Williams who lived at Borough Fen survives. He was almost certainly named John. Each generation of the family contained a John, and it is always difficult and sometimes impossible, in the absence of dates, to determine to which John reference is being made. But he lived at the decoy with his son, also a John, of whom fairly complete records have survived.

43

THE WILLIAMS FAMILY TREE

The names of those associated with decoys and the decoys with which they were associated are in capitals.

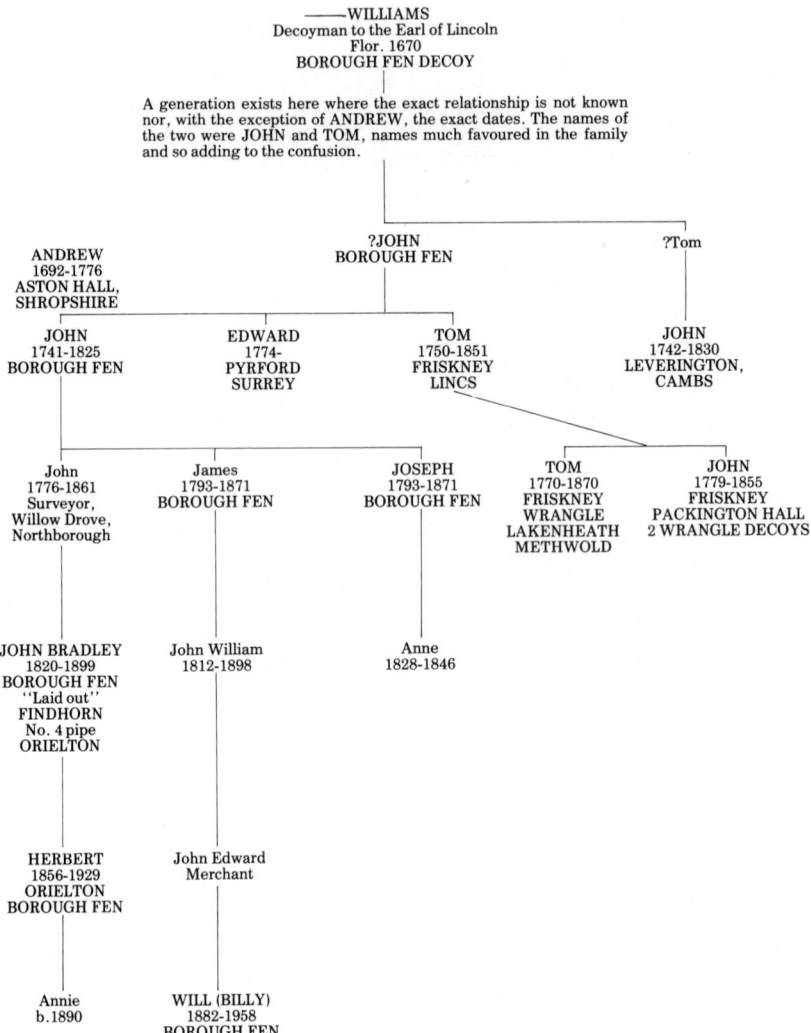

————WILLIAMS
Decoyman to the Earl of Lincoln
Flor. 1670
BOROUGH FEN DECOY

A generation exists here where the exact relationship is not known nor, with the exception of ANDREW, the exact dates. The names of the two were JOHN and TOM, names much favoured in the family and so adding to the confusion.

ANDREW
1692-1776
ASTON HALL,
SHROPSHIRE

?JOHN
BOROUGH FEN

?Tom

JOHN
1741-1825
BOROUGH FEN

EDWARD
1774-
PYRFORD
SURREY

TOM
1750-1851
FRISKNEY
LINCS

JOHN
1742-1830
LEVERINGTON,
CAMBS

John
1776-1861
Surveyor,
Willow Drove,
Northborough

James
1793-1871
BOROUGH FEN

JOSEPH
1793-1871
BOROUGH FEN

TOM
1770-1870
FRISKNEY
WRANGLE
LAKENHEATH
METHWOLD

JOHN
1779-1855
FRISKNEY
PACKINGTON HALL
2 WRANGLE DECOYS

JOHN BRADLEY
1820-1899
BOROUGH FEN
"Laid out"
FINDHORN
No. 4 pipe
ORIELTON

John William
1812-1898

Anne
1828-1846

HERBERT
1856-1929
ORIELTON
BOROUGH FEN

John Edward
Merchant

Annie
b.1890

WILL (BILLY)
1882-1958
BOROUGH FEN

John Williams was born at Decoy Farm in 1741. Alarge portrait of him, in oils and believed to have been painted about 1800, shows a man of distiction and authority. His grey eyes look straight at one in a frank, intelligent gaze. There is nothing of the furtive decoyman about him but the look of a man who enjoys good living and the company of his fellow men.

He was one of the most skilful workers of the decoy and, in his early days, nothing was allowed to interfere with his management of it. A story is told of a cousin who had come to stay at the farm house in early winter in order to learn the art of catching ducks. Weeks went by and no attempt had been made to catch any ducks. Nothing would go right; first there were no ducks, then there was no wind and then the pond became frozen over. Then, on the afternoon of Christmas Day, when the whole family was sitting round the dinner table and the goose had just been brought in, waiting for father to start carving it, in walked John. "Now, my dear cousin," he said, "now is the exact time". The younger John had to go out immediately into the decoy. The time was indeed right. They caught a very large number of ducks but they came back to a cold and spoiled Christmas dinner. It has become a tradition now for one of the family to repeat the remark, "Now is the exact time, my dear cousin", when the Christmas goose is laid before them on the table.

John of the portrait was the first of the family to serve as an Officer and Surveyor to the Commissioners of the Bedford Level and it was he who laid out the straight intersecting roads between the east bank of the Welland and Clough's Cross near Wisbech; under his direction, too, most of the straight dykes which drain the North Level were cut. He was also the tenant of Decoy Farm and in his later years farming and surveying occupied so much of his time that he had to have regular help in the decoy. Records of his catches for a number of years survive, but they are not, unfortunately, complete. In 1776-77, the first season of which there is record, he had an exceptionally good year, catching 4,857 ducks. Three years later the catch was only about fifty and in the following year only a little better. The cause of these bad years when the fens should have been teeming with ducks is not known. There are many possibilities. Major repairs including the cleaning of the pond may have been carried out. He may have been ill. More probably by now farming and surveying had proved more profitable than decoying and were taking up his time and interest. After those poor years he employed, in 1789, a decoyman and with his help the catches improved until in 1804-5 he made the biggest catch ever recorded, 450 dozen and 8. Exactly how many birds that involved it is impossible to say for all ducks other than Mallard counted as half-ducks and one dozen could mean 12 Mallard or 24 Teal. But at the lowest estimate, if they were all Mallard, there were 5,408 ducks.

45

Mallard were at this time making 3/2d (16p) each and although this was a peak year as regards number of birds taken, it was not a peak year as regards price. In 1810, during the blockade of the Napoleonic wars, the price of a Mallard soared to 4/9½d (24p) a bird, a price which his dealer appears to have been only too pleased to give him. He sold his birds to a Mr Samuel Boyce of London, who wrote - the spelling is his - on September 2nd 1789, "Inclosed is your Acct. which I hope you will find Wright. I should have sent it before but was in hopes I could have time to make a journey to Peterboro. However I do not Quite give up the Thought of Coming as I could wish to see you and my friend Bowen also before Winter Comes on. I am in your debt 2; 15; 0 which I will pay on Demand pray give my respect to yr. Brothers and Family and your self from your Humle Servant, Samuel Boyce".

Probably because of the authority associated with his position as an Officer of the Commissioners of the North Level he was chosen by his landlord to act in an official position for him also. He published a notice with, under the word "Caution" in very heavy block capitals the following - "Whereas the Wash Lands in the Parishes of Newborough, Northamptonshire and Deeping St. James, Lincolnshire, belonging to Sir Culling Eardley Eardley, Bart., have of late been much trespassed upon by persons Shooting and Fishing. This is to give notice that the Tenant has received strict orders from Sir Culling Eardley Eardley to prosecute all such Offenders to the utmost rigour of the Law". John Williams, Borough Fen. Tenant.

There survives a document in his very neat handwriting which reads -
"Of wild ducks, wild geese and other water fowl. Every person who shall shoot at, kill or destroy with any gun or bow, any Mallard, Duck, Teal or Widgeon, and the same be proved by confefsion, or oath of two witnefses, before two Justices, shall be Committed to gaol for three months, unlefs he pay to the Churchwardens for the use of the poor 20/- or after one month after committment become bound by recognifance with two sureties before two Justices, in £20 each not to offend again in like manner, which recognifance shall be returned to the next sefsions".

He died in 1825, a wealthy man. In his will, in which he is described as "Gentleman, of Borough Fen", after leaving sums of money to his three sons and two daughters "for all of whom I have already provided", he left the residue of his estate of just under £3,000 to his youngest son Joseph.

An Obituary Notice in the Lincoln, Stamford and Rutland Mercury for April 29th 1825 reads - "On Wednesday the 20th inst., at the Decoy, Borough Fen, Mr. Williams, aged 84. He was a kind and indulgent parent and master; a generous and hospitable friend and neighbour; and a peaceful, upright and virtuous man''.

The John Williams above had two younger brothers who worked in decoys, the elder, Edward, being born at the decoy farm in 1744 and Tom in 1750. Little is known of Edward other than he worked the Pyrford Decoy, near Woking in Surrey, for a number of years. This was not a new decoy at the time of his arrival but had been according to Sir Ralph Payne-Gallwey, "originally the property of Sir John Wooley, Latin Secretary to Queen Elizabeth, who provided himself on having within his own estate every possible appliance for the provision of his table, and the wants of his household. Thus, not far from the decoy, is a place called the Pigeon House, and there are still signs of the sluices which were cut from the old bed of the River Wey which here forms almost an island on all sides of it, save to the north''.

The youngest of the three brothers, Tom, was born in 1750. After helping in the decoy and learning his trade there, he left Borough Fen in 1770 and settled in Friskney in Lincolnshire building a decoy there in what was then the heart of the decoy country. He married a local girl and stayed there for the remainder of his long life. He died on May 27th 1851 at the age of 101. He was buried at Friskney churchyard at the side of his wife Martha who at the age of 87 died some years before him.

On his gravestone is written, in addition to his age and date of birth and death, the following lines -
He was an Honest and Inoffensive Friend,
Peaceful in Life and Happy in his End.
In all his Dealings Just,
Faithful to his Friends and to his Trust.

He had two sons, Thomas and John, who at first worked their father's decoy, but when owing to the effects of the drainage of the East and West Fens this became unprofitable, moved a few miles south to Wrangle where they worked two decoys, the one nearer the sea being known for many years as "Old Tom's Decoy''.

In 1795 John was employed by the Earl of Aylesford in building for him a decoy at Packington Hall, Warwickshire. It was of a kind which must have been strange to John for it lay with its four pipes at the end of a lake of 30 acres. It was never used commercially but only to provide birds for the Earl's table. When this was done John returned to Lincolnshire where he died in 1855 at the age of 76. He was buried in Friskney churchyard near his father.

Meanwhile Tom, when the same fate had overtaken his Wrangle Decoy as had his Friskney one, moved on to Lakenheath on the Norfolk-Suffolk border, where he worked a decoy for a Mr Eagle. It is reported that in one year he "cleared near £700 on sale of duck taken at Lakenheath'' and that ''he used to send up a ton of ducks to London twice a week in the season''. An old keeper living in the parish in 1878 declared that once he saw fully 3,000 fowl sitting outside the decoy in the fen ''waiting for those inside to be taken to make room for them, as the Decoy was so full it looked as if one could not prick a pin in anywhere''. The decoy was abandoned in 1855 for reasons unknown and Tom moved to Methwold, where Mrs Wilson, widow of the late tenant, employed him as a decoyman. Her brother, Mr Harwin, later took over the decoy but kept Tom on, very wisely, for ''on one occasion, a thaw having set in, the fowl coming in from the coast very hungry, Williams drove up 75 Wild Ducks, all at once, the most he ever saw taken at one time. He saw 50 and 60 taken many times''.

Tom would often ride over from Lakenheath to Borough Fen to see his uncle John. On one of these visits, the exact date of which is not known but was probably about 1810, he brought over in a flagon basket a small oak tree which was planted just outside the decoy on the south side of the approach path. This has now grown into a splendid tree, a memorial to this remarkable man.

He died in 1870 at the age of 100, when he fell into a fen ditch one frosty moonlit night, with a load of ducks on his back, and was drowned. In his lifetime he became a legendary figure and after his death the imagination of his many admirers tried to add unnecessary to his stature. His age at death has been given variously as 107 and 109. The uncertainty may have arisen partly from confusion with his long-lived father who had the same christian name. More probably, he himself did not know the year of his birth. Reference to Parish Registers has confirmed the date of his death but not of his birth and the subtraction of a few years from such longevity has done nothing to diminish the fame of this magnificent centenarian.

After Tom's death Mr Harwin managed the decoy hinself for two years. He said his fortune was not as good as formerly but he considered duck-catching was nice amusement, although working the decoy was very trying in frosty weather. Mr Harwin was like many other people. From the outside decoying seemed easy money. Only those who have tried it know the patience, the skill and the hardiness which are required to make a decoy pay its way.

The younger John, the hero of the story of the spoiled Christmas dinner, went to Leverington Decoy, near Wisbech. He profited so much by his cousin's advice and example, that he was able to give up his decoy in 1782, when he took farms at Postland and Crowland bought out of his savings. The Deed of Possession reads ''Be it remembered that I Thomas Porter of Hygh Borrow Fens in the County of Northampton Have this Day let unto John Williams of Leverington on the Oyle of Eley Decoyman, all my Farms in

48

Postland in the Parrish of Crowland, containing 200 Acres more or less, at the yearly rent of 140 pounds each yeare...".

Thomas Porter agreed to pay John Williams "a sum of 20 pounds in consideration of the Said Farme being in Bad repareness". John appears to have got the farm into good condition. A Bill of Sale survives in which it states that a John Wrigglesworth "bought of John Williams forty stones of hemp, (weighing fourteen pounds to each stone), that was grown on a piece of Land containing two acres, in his tenure, in the Parish of Crowland in the County of Lincoln, and in the year 1784".

Joseph Williams, the youngest child of John Williams, was born in 1793. At the age of 14 he was apprenticed to an elder brother, James Williams of Crowland, a grocer and tallow chandler, "to learn the Art and with him (after the manner of an apprentice) to serve from the first day of October one thousand eight hundred and seven unto the Full End and Term of Seven Years, from thence next following to be compleat and ended". The Indenture contains many restrictions on the young apprentice's activities. "The said Apprentice his Master faithfully shall serve, his Secrets keep, his lawful Commands everywhere shall do. He shall not contract matrimony, within the said term. He shall not play at Cards, Dice, Tables or any other unlawful Games whereby his said Master may have any loss. He shall not haunt Taverns or Playhouses, nor absent himself from his said Master's service Day or Night unlawfully". In return for Joseph's services James was to "teach and instruct in the Art of a Grocer and Tallow 'Chandler, finding the said Apprentice sufficient Meat, Drink and Washing and Lodging during the said Term". His father did "hereby agree to find and provide his said Son with Sufficient Clothing during the said Term". The Indenture bears the signatures of his father, his brother James and Joseph himself.

He completed his term of apprenticeship in 1815, but there is no record of how long he continued in the trade of grocer and tallow chandler. It seems probably that he stayed in Crowland for a few years, but with his thoughts returning constantly to his home, the farm and the decoy, he spent more and more time in Borough Fen. It is most unlikely that decoying was a new and strange art when, ten years after completing his apprenticeship, he inherited from his father. Records in the first two years after he took over are at least as good as the average and in the next four years his catches were exceptionally large. It is probable that his great interest in the decoy was the reason for his father leaving it to him, the youngest son, when he and his other brothers were in full employment.

Both the farm and decoy prospered. In 1829 he was able to lease a part of the Welland Bank at Crowland and to build a house thereon, property which remains in the Williams family's hands to this day.

The Lease was forwarded "by direction of Mr. Wells of the Boston Evening Coach", and was to be signed in the presence of one witness and then returned with a Register's fee of five guineas".

He also had his troubles. Mindful, no doubt, of the successful conclusion of the case Keeble v. Hickeringall, he sued in 1829 a Mr Seaton who had deliberately disturbed the decoy and driven the ducks away. He received on February 20th 1830 a letter, written in Spalding, which read -

Sir,
    I beg to inform you that Mr. Seaton has this day paid us £5 for the penalty incurred for disturbing your Decoy, also our costs.
                                        I am Sir, your obedient Servant,
                                            Saml. Edwards, Senior.

He appears, also, to have had a disagreement with his landlord for the following year, on October 6th, he received this rather curt note -

Sir,
    Sir C. Smith says he has no objection to the Rent of £100 a year for the *Decoy,* but he will have no expense in maintaining the wood nor in clearing out the Decoy pond the first year. If the Decoy had been properly tenanted, it ought not to require it.

    Pray ride over here on Monday if you possibly can, that Sir. C. may know if the terms are acceptable by you.
                                        I am, Sir,
                                    Your obed. servant.
                                        G.W. Simonds.

Joseph presumably accepted the terms in this letter for he continued to live at the decoy farm. In 1835, however, he received another letter from his landlord, Sir Culling Eardley Smith, Bart., which contained a notice to "quit and leave the Possession, on the twenty-fifth of March or so soon after as your holding shall expire, of all the Messuages, Farms, Lands, Tenements and Hereditaments, which you hold of me, situate in Borough Fen in the County of Northampton and elsewhere: and I also give you Notice to leave the same in a proper state of Repair and Cultivation. Dated this twenty-third Day of September one thousand eight hundred and thirty five". The letter was signed by Sir Culling.

50

It is not known what prompted this second letter and whether there were further disagreements between Joseph and his landlord. There may be a kinder explanation for shortly after this letter was written Sir Culling's estate was broken up and the ownership of the property was transferred to his daughter, Mrs S.F. Culling Hanbury. Joseph certainly continued to live at the decoy farm, for on January 1st 1851 he signed a lease with his landlord of 127 acres 1½ roods, which included farmland and the decoy at an annual rent of £271. 16s. 0d. The lease was for twenty-one years.

Complete records of his catches after 1840 are lost, but there are several discontinuous records of isolated catches and the prices the ducks made at market. These give some insight into the economics of decoying at that time. At the end of March 1849 he had been paid £163. 18s. 4d for ducks caught ''at the end of the season''. In 1853 the ducks he had caught between November 1st and December 21st brought in, after paying commission, the sum of £82. 8s. 1d., and on December 30th Mr. Christopher Thorne of Leadenhall Market acknowledged the receipt of another hamper of birds in a letter in which he said — ''not many of the last lot of fowl sold as they are very thin''. However the hamper made £23. When sending the money for the last sale, Mr. Thorne wrote ''There has been so much foreign trade over that it is hard to sell at all. The market is now as full as possible and the prices will be bad as none was wanted at Christmas''. It appears that the problems facing the home producers at that time from foreign dumping on the market were much as they are today for birds were being imported in large numbers from the Dutch decoys. However, things looked up at the turn of the year and in January, February and March, when the season closed, Mr. Thorne was able to sell £50 worth of ducks each month, and it is clear from the records of catches, where they exist, that he was only getting a proportion of Joseph's birds. On the back of the last acknowledgement of the receipt of birds, on March 21st, he wrote, not very grammatically, ''As the Season is over now and am very pleased (for both of us) that it has been a better one. We have payed the money into the Banks as before. Yours Truly, Chris Thorne''.

At this time Mallard were making 1/2d. to 1/5d. (6 to 7p) each, Pintail were making 1/- (5p), Wigeon 8d. (3p), Shoveler (which Mr. Thorne spelt ''Shuffler'') 8d. and Teal 6½d. (2½p).

Besides the decoy Joseph also inherited from his father a horse, of which a painting survives. In the bottom right hand corner of this picture there is a note that it died in 1828 at the age of 32. The horse had been used to take a load of ducks, as required, to Norman Cross on the Great North Road, some 16 miles away.

Life at the decoy farm house appears to have been a very happy and sociable one. Joseph's wife, Ann, of whom a miniature survives, was a large, generous woman, content to have the family and her friends around her. She was a great cook with the frying of pancakes her special delight. At pancake parties, which she loved to hold at frequent intervals, her only child, Anne, the many cousins in the Williams family, and her special friends such as the Griffins and the Vergettes, would all sit together in the large kitchen, eating pancakes and making nets to cover the decoy pipes. Good living and a happy disposition, as often happens, played havoc with her figure and she became very fat. It is said that when Sir Culling Eardley Smith's agent called one day he asked her how much she weighed. Twenty-two stone net, she replied. Was net, he asked, with or without her clothes? In, presumably, her slimmer days, she was accustomed to ride to market side-saddle on the horse behind her husband. Once when he returned home, he called to his wife to dismount. When there was no reply he turned round and found no Ann. In great distress he rode back and several miles away he found a bruised but still smiling Ann limping her way home.

There is a portrait of Joseph, the date of which is not known. It shows a neat, dapper little man, good natured and not one likely to fall out with his landlord. Farming occupied so much of his time that he, like his father, had for the last forty years of his tenure to employ a decoyman, one Charlie Smith, who outlived his master by twenty years. He appears to have been a man of exceptional energy and hardiness. He would during the night go round the decoy time and time again in a blizzard, making sure that the weight of snow did not break the wooden hoops and bring the nets down. Long before dawn he would be down at the decoy breaking ice in a hard spell before the ducks returned at first light. It is a pity that such incomplete records survive of those years in which he made his great catches.

Joseph continued to live at the decoy until his death in 1871. Many of his letters and documents survive together with his own portrait and that of his wife and his horse. In his will he left a large number of bequests to members of the family and his friends and ''a sum of forty pounds free of duty to my foreman, Charles Smith of Peakirk''. The residue of his estate, together with certain sums of money, he left to his nephew John Bradley Williams and his wife Sarah.

There was only one child of the marriage, a daughter, Anne, born in 1828. She was sent to a boarding school in Market Deeping under the care of the Misses Smith. A sampler, which she worked at the age of eight, shows, in view of her age, very great skill and patience, but probably even more remarkable is a letter which she wrote to her parents a year later.

My dear Parents,

With great and sincere pleasure I write to tell you that the Christmas holidays will commence on Friday, the 15th. of the month, when I hope to see you and all my friends in perfect health, and I think I shall enjoy myself very much with you all. Hope that the improvement that I have made in my learning since Mid-summer will meet with your kind approbation.

I have finished one half of my mother's collar and begun the other, and hope she will like it. I should like to know when my cousin Emma and Elizabeth's holidays commence. I am very much obliged for Mrs. Elliott's invitation and hope you will let me go. Mrs. Richmond has been so kind as to ask me to go and spend a week or a fortnight with Miss Richmond.

Please give my love to my father and accept the same for yourself from your dutiful and affectionate daughter.

Anne Williams

The letter, beautifully written and clearly very much a "fair copy" is a credit to both Anne and her teachers. It sounds today somewhat priggish and precocious for a child of just nine, but it gives a true picture of the manners and discipline of a child at the beginning of Queen Victoria's reign.

Joseph and his wife were soon to lose their only child. At the age of 19, in the year 1846, she went to visit her sweetheart, who lived near Wisbech and was ill with a fever. He survived but Anne caught the fever and died. Many years later an old man came to visit the decoy. He said he was Anne's sweetheart and that he had never been to the decoy since her death. He wished to see it once more he, too, died.

John Bradley Williams was born in 1820. He was the son of John Williams, the Surveyor and Joseph's eldest brother, and grandson of John Williams (1745 — 1825). He lived in Willow Drove, the road to the east of the decoy, and he followed his father and grandfather as Surveyor and Officer to the Commissioners of the Bedford Level, having charge of a large area of land between the Welland and Clough's Cross near Wisbech. He appears to have been also a rate collector and bailiff. A notice, dated December 1st 1846, reads — "Take Notice. Any person or persons found Cutting, Taking away or otherwise Destroying the wood growing in the Holts by the side of the West Bank near the Town of Crowland, belonging to the Honourable Corporation of the Bedford Level will be prosecuted according to the Law.

Any person giving information of the Offenders to Mr. Robert Harker Constable of Crowland so that they may be brought to Justice shall receive a reward of One Guinea from John Williams, Officer to the Said Honourable Corporation''.

When he moved to the decoy farm in the spring of 1871 one of his first acts was to have the pond cleaned out. There is a receipt, dated September 27th 1871 for the sum of £2. 5s. 0d. (£2.25) paid ''for the use of 3 dobin carts, 5 weeks at 9s. a week''. He had also inherited a farm of 127 acres and this with his official work occupied so much of his time that he was forced to leave much of the practical work in the decoy to Charlie Smith who had served his uncle Joseph so well. It would appear, indeed, that he was more interested in the art and theory of decoying rather than in the practice, and in designing decoys rather than working them.

He ''set out'', to use his own phrase, the No.4 pipe at Orielton Decoy in Pembrokeshire, which was worked in its early years by his son, Herbert. He also ''set out'' a decoy ''in Scotland near Findhorn Bay'' for Major R. Chadwick. This was begun but never completed.

He has left a list of known decoys, based apparently on Payne-Gallwey's book, but with his own comments in the margin, mostly when one of the Williams family was involved. At the end of the list, among other notes, he has written — ''Stafford for Sir G. Pigot: built by Uncle Edward and worked by Uncle Tom''. No record can be found of this decoy and it is probably that ''Stafford'' should read ''Pyrford'', a decoy near Woking, which was owned by Mr. George Pigot. At the time that he was writing, the decoy had been out of use for many years. Uncle Edward, was in fact, his great uncle.

Although he left a number of notes on decoys, a working plan of No.4 pipe at Orielton, a drawing of part of Findhorn Decoy and designs for other decoys, he kept few records of his catches. He sold his birds to E. and W.H. Davis, who describe themselves on the invoice as nephews of the late Christopher Horne. In March 1870 the firm, enclosing a sum of £36. 5s. 0d. wrote — ''Wild Ducks are in demand, awaiting further favours''. They paid him 3/- (15p) for a Mallard; Wigeon and Teal made 1/- (5p) each, very good prices for those days.

Only records of occasional months survive. In October 1888 he caught 409 Mallard, 617 Teal and 40 Wigeon. In the January of the following year he caught 353 Mallard, 18 Teal and 1 Wigeon, with 337 Mallard, 3 Pintail, 11 Teal and 15 Wigeon in the following month. His catches in 1889 and 1890 were rather smaller but in February 1891 he caught 591 Mallard, 61 Teal, 14 Pintail and 64 Wigeon.

He also had his troubles from disturbance of the decoy. He

54

published a notice saying "Gentlemen are requested not to course or shoot on Land in the occupation of John B. Williams in Borough Fen and Newborough Fen and Deeping St. James' Washes. Anyone firing a Gun whereby the Wildfowl may be raised in the Decoy in Borough Fen will be held liable in damages and costs". The notice appears to have been effective and no prosecution became necessary

John Bradley Williams had four sons and many daughters. His eldest son, John Randall, helped with the farm but died at the age of 30. His second son, Frederick, farmed for a time in the fen and then emigrated to New Zealand. His third son, Herbert, after a few years in the decoy at Orielton, returned to Borough Fen where he helped his father on the farm and in the decoy. The fourth son, Robert, became, like his father, a Surveyor and Officer to the Commissioners. His many daughters all married, but some of them, he considered, not well, so that he made large contributions to their upkeep in order that they should not fall below the social standing of their parents.

He is remembered as a heavily built man with a long black beard; a severe man, much on his dignity. He was the classical Victorian head of the family, very much the master in his own house, ruling the family with a rod of iron. After family prayers, which everyone in the house was made to attend, he issued his orders for the day, orders which were invariably obeyed. He was probably the most intellectually accomplished of all the family that lived in Borough Fen, but he was not the most likeable. He died in 1899 in his eightieth year.

Herbert, John Bradley Williams' third son, went to Pembrokeshire at the age of 20 to supervise the building of the fourth pipe at Orielton and he stayed a few years working this decoy. He then returned to Borough Fen where he remained for the rest of his days.

He had inherited his father's efficiency with none of his pomposity. The decoy became his life. During his father's tenancy he laid out gardens at the farm house and in the decoy new paths bordered by flowering shrubs and climbing roses appeared, so that the decoy lost some of its austerity but none of its effectiveness. The pipes and the screens were immaculately kept and the paths carefully levelled and mown. He delighted to open the decoy during the close season to his many friends and to hold parties there and even fetes in aid of charities or the church in what had become a woodland oasis in a highly cultivated countryside. Intensely social as he was, there was much else to do in the few months of the close season beside entertaining his friends and all the maintenance and repair work must always be finished by the first week in July. After that the gates were closed and locked and no-one must enter. With Arthur Hill, his decoyman, he had seen the first few ducks fly in and they had stayed all day. Nothing must be allowed to disturb them or spoil their sense of security, for these were his "lead in", birds which would leave the pond each evening and at dawn bring other ducks with them when they returned.

When the catching season came round again he made no unnecessary visit. He did not believe in the "little and often" principle, that by frequent visits and frequent small catches a large total would eventually be reached. On very many days he would not go near the decoy. Occasionally he would go in, generally at about 10 o'clock in the morning, when the ducks, well-fed during the night and now washed, were sleepy and not easily disturbed. He would see how many there were and where they lay, and he would go away and wait. Then one day he would look at the wind and look at the clouds, he would go into the house and warn everyone to be quiet and then, taking a burning peat sod, he would collect his decoyman, Hill, and his dog and together they would steal silently into the decoy and to the pipe appropriate to the wind. There he would make one of his big catches. His favourite time for a catch was 3 p.m. on an autumn or winter's day, when the ducks were well rested and beginning to feel hungry. His best catch was 404 ducks in one pipe in one day.

Unfortunately, like his father and so many of his predecessors, he did not in his early days keep complete records of his catches and only records of certain months survive. His records only became complete from 1913 onwards. Only one season, 1804-05, when the fens must have been teeming with ducks, surpasses his good years, 1913-24. In 1919-20 he caught 5,064 ducks. The best recorded season is 1804-05 when the catch was 5,408 ducks; in only one season, other than this, has the 4,000 been exceeded.

He was probably the greatest decoyman of this great family. His success was due to his meticulous attention to detail on every occasion. Whenever he went into the decoy he would always take a piece of burning peat with him. This was based on the theory that the ducks by haunting cultivated fields at night, often near the farm cottages, and often flying over those cottages, were familiar with the smell of the fuel most cottagers burnt at that time; the smell drifting across them as they swam on the pond caused them no alarm and would drown the smell of human beings. This was probably a fallacy for it is not certain that ducks have such a keen sense of smell. More probably the composure of the birds was due to another factor. He would never pass upwind of the birds, when the possibility of hearing him would be at least as great as their smelling him. Although in his later years a heavily-built man, he could at all times move with the utmost stealth and every twig was removed from the path before him in case the noise of the twig snapping under foot alarmed the ducks. His daughter recalls how one day

56

when the wind was blowing from the farm to the pond, he came into the house and went into the kitchen in a rage at the smell of burning, not worrying that it might be the smell of his dinner spoiling, but that it might alarm the ducks.

For a number of years he farmed the fields around the decoy with his brother Fred, but in 1913 Colonel Fremantle, the owner at that time, sold the estate to the Olympia Oil Company and Fred emigrated to New Zealand. Later the land and much more around it was bought from the company and after the first World War made into small holdings.

Herbert died in 1929, leaving one daughter, Annie. Among his many accomplishments was his skill as an ice skater. Crowland and Cowbit Washes, in the days when they flooded each winter and frequently became frozen over, would attract skaters from all over Britain for the Fenland Championships. A Fenland Champion was virtually a champion of Britain. It was one of Herbert's proudest moments when as a young man he won the one mile championship of the Fens.

There are many who remember him, the kindest and the most hospitable of men, immensely proud of his decoy and the family traditions. Anyone who loved the decoy was his friend and everyone who knew him sought his friendship.

Billy Williams, the last of this long line of decoymen, was born on December 27th 1882 in Crowland where his father, John Edward Williams, was a baker and confectioner and where he went to school. He was the great-great-grandson of John Williams.

On leaving school he joined his father in business, but times were bad and the neighbourhood, essentially agricultural, was in a state of depression. In 1903, like many young men at that time, he took advantage of a government settlement scheme and emigrated to Canada where he joined his eldest brother, Edward, who had gone out a few years previously. There, in Saskatchewan, they had a ranch of 160 acres, mostly recovered by them from the virgin forest. The life was hard, so much had to be accomplished in the short summers and in the bitter cold of the long winters there was little that could be done on the ranch and he used to join various lumber camps. It was while he was working in one of these camps that a frozen axe handle slipped in his numbed fingers and he struck his foot, almost completely severing his toes. Some of the lumbermen advised an immediate journey to hospital 40 miles away while others suggested various remedies. An old half-caste French Canadian Indian trapper said, "You go to hospital, you lose your money, you lose your toes. Stay with Francois, you save your money, you save your toes". Billy stayed. The trapper treated the wounds with a concoction of birch bark and sphagnum moss and the wounds eventually healed. Although he was left with a very stiff forefoot the injury caused him until his latter years few symptoms but it did cause an otherwise very fit man to be graded C3 when he went before a medical board during the first World War, and he was not called up for service until 1917.

For a time Billy and his brother struggled on but the ranch was, they felt, too far north. Too frequently an early winter spoilt much of their crops and, in 1909, when a particularly early winter spoiled a complete harvest, Billy was persuaded to return home and join another brother who had set up in business as a corn, pea and produce merchant in Crowland. The business prospered but in 1917 he was called up. He joined the army and did most of his service in Mesopotamia.

He returned to Britain in 1920 and was demobilised. He married that year his cousin Annie and he went to live at the decoy farm with his father and mother-in-law, Mr. and Mrs. Herbert Williams. He had had until then no knowledge or experience of work in a decoy but he was a man with an active, enquiring mind, interested in all aspects of nature and with a strong hunting interest. His life in Canada had accustomed him to working with his hands and to making do with nearby natural materials and he soon acquired an expert skill in the enormous amount of maintenance work entailed in a decoy. He could have had no better tutor than his father-in-law in the art of catching ducks. When, therefore, in 1929 Herbert Williams died, Billy was well able, with the assistance of the old decoy-hand Hill, to take over the decoy. Ten years later, Hill, now an old man, left him and Billy was on his own, rather to his relief. No longer would he be told when ducks they had been hoping to take flew out of a pipe, "they 'eard you" — it was always "you" for no duck had ever been known to have heard Hill — or when he acted, often on Hill's advice, that "that was no way to set about the job".

The take in the decoy gradually improved after the poor year in 1927 and the numbers continued to increase after Hill's departure but they never reached his father-in-law's best years. For a time he used a cat to bring the birds in, dropping it over the dog leap, and the ducks would respond well to it, coming freely up the pipe, but it was not as amenable to discipline, too independent, he used to say, and he then used a white smooth-haired terrier, Spot. When Spot died, he used two yellow labradors, Nella and Amber.

Nothing brought Billy greater joy than when killing the birds he caught became no longer necessary for his livelihood. When he had had to kill, death came instantaneously, the neck being broken close to the skull. He locked the wings over their backs and the birds lay still without flapping, for a flapping bird soon disarranged and dirtied its plumage. A merchant once said to him "Mr Williams, your birds always look as though they died in their sleep''. Because of their immaculate condition decoy-caught birds always made more at market than shot ones. He would say in defence of decoying that, as opposed to shooting, there were no wounded and crippled birds to fly away and die, probably in misery. His joy was in the hunt, in the bringing to a successful conclusion an exercise that demanded knowledge, skill and patience. That conclusion would now be without bloodshed and the decoy would no longer carry the opprobrious stigma of an ''antiquated slaughter house'', as it had once been called. From now on he could sit in peace of mind in the hut over-looking the pond, watching the birds which in his heart he loved. Now they would pay no penalty for being caught other than the wearing of a ring round one leg, a matter apparently of no hardship. For a short time after its release a bird tends to fly with the ringed leg hanging down, as birds do when a lump of mud sticks to a foot, but the leg is soon drawn up and they behave normally. Indeed, unless one can actually see the ring, it is generally impossible to tell which in a group of birds is carrying a ring.

When the scheme was first started in 1949 Billy was paid at market prices for all the Teal and the few Shoveler and Pintail he caught and released. There were then insufficient funds to pay for the more expensive Mallard and they were sent to market. Then in 1954 Mallard were also included and no more birds were killed. The annual take during his management are not wholly comparable with those of his predecessors, for apart from the fact that until 1949 there were no recaptures or recoveries (for all birds were killed), problems arose in the actual catching of the ducks. If a duck had been caught once, or possibly twice - although some ducks were caught three or four times and one even three times on one day - it was generally reluctant to enter a pipe again and so, after a time, a large number of the ducks on the pond had been caught at least once. The entrance to a pipe became thronged with birds reluctant to enter and fresh birds, sensing the disquiet of their experienced fellows, also hung about the entrance and were difficult to catch The birds became more quickly what the old decoyman called ''stale''.

The subsequent history of his recoveries was a matter of great interest to Billy and he was always delighted to meet up with an old friend, possibly a bird he had caught some years before. One instance in particular gave him great pleasure. It was a Heron, not a duck, and the first Heron he had caught. Having no special ring for Herons, he put a Mallard-size ring on its leg and it appeared to be a satisfactory fit. He released the bird with his blessing and duly recorded the capture at the British Museum, where at that time records of all recoveries were sent. He got in reply a rebuke for applying to a bird a ring which must have been unsuitable and might cause distress. Duly chastened he continued to catch and ring Mallard until in the following year he found one morning a Heron in a pipe. He caught it and to his surprise he found it was the same Heron he had caught in the same pipe the previous year. He examined the ringed leg with some anxiety but to his relief there was no evidence of soreness of the bird's leg, the ring seemed to fit perfectly and was not unduly worn. He released the bird and was able to write to the authority that the bird had reported again for examination and, if necessary, a refit of its ring, but that everything appeared to be satisfactory. The bird was allowed to continue on its way.

His most amusing recovery concerned a Mallard. An anxious correspondent wrote a letter to the **Field**, saying that he had sent to the British Museum a ring which he had recovered from a pork pie served him in a London restaurant. He asked the Museum, since the ring was theirs, to let him know "what beast had escaped from their care" to find its way onto his luncheon plate. He was told that the ring came from the leg of a Mallard, a bird Billy had caught, ringed and released, but which had been shot shortly afterwards.

In 1939 the decoy, the farm house and much surrounding land, none of which had any member of the Williams family at any time owned, changed hands. Billy was given a lease of the decoy and the house where he and Annie lived. In 1949 the farm house was needed by the new owner and they went to live on the Glinton Road, Peakirk, from where Billy continued to work the decoy. On New Year's Day of the following year a heavy snowstorm brought down all the pipes and the decoy became unworkable for the rest of the season. A difficult summer followed but all the pipes were repaired, new screens built and much new netting applied. Then, in 1951, he had a severe illness during which for a time he suffered an almost complete loss of his eyesight and he was unable to visit the decoy for many months.

Gradually as his health improved his luck seemed to change.He was encouraged by the fact that he had no longer to kill all the ducks he caught in order to obtain a livelihood and he was assured of a more steady income. In 1955 an old stone-built thatched cottage, part of it bearing the date 1730, together with about 5 acres of land was purchased at Peakirk and this together with some old gravel beds and an osier holt, the relic of an old basket-making factory, became the nucleus of the present Waterfowl Gardens of the Wildfowl Trust, and before they were opened to the public, to his great delight, Billy became their first curator. In 1956 he was joined by Tony Cook, at first on a part-time basis, who was able later to relieve him of most of the routine work at the decoy. The Goshams in its attractive setting, a village green in front, flanked by tall elms and beyond, St. Pega's church; at the back the waterfowl gardens, gradually became the centre of his life, but never to the exclusion of Borough Fen Decoy.

Sir Ralph Payne-Gallwey's description of a typical decoyman, doubtless true in his day, bears little resemblance to Billy Williams. A decoyman, Sir Ralph wrote, lived a quiet lonely life, seldom attending fairs or markets. He was always on the watch for intruders and would on no account give them the slightest reliable information. Secretive and unsociable, he was at pains to keep the working of his decoy in mystery, giving nothing away and keeping his successes in secret lest some covetous neighbour, jealous of his profits, set up for himself a decoy hard by, so robbing him of half his profits. In contrast, one remembers Billy as a man with a smile on his face, a humorous twinkle in his blue eyes and, as Sir Peter Scott wrote in *The Eye of the Wind,* a robin-like welcome. He was intensely sociable and enjoyed the company of his fellow men; only Herbert and his wife can have equalled his and Annie's hospitality. Far from being secretive he was ever willing to discuss the technique of catching ducks, and in the close season to show people round the decoy grounds of which he was so immensely proud. Only when the catching season approached or had started was the absolute privacy of the decoy jealously guarded.

Few men can have had a wider circle of friends who were delighted to listen to his tales, for he was an excellent raconteur, tales of his life in Canada, of his experiences in the decoy, and of the people of the surrounding countryside whom he knew and understood so well, people who were the descendants of those fenmen who had been such a thorn in the flesh of successive Abbots of Crowland and who (in a few instances) appeared to have done little to mend their ways.

Billy died in 1958 and was buried at Peakirk in the churchyard of St Pega within sight of his native Crowland and its Abbey of St Guthlac, St Pega's brother, and the tall trees of his decoy. At his funeral service people from all parts of the country filled the church and, overflowing into the churchyard, stood bare-headed among the tombstones of the many Williams who over a span of three centuries had been laid in their native fenland soil.

He is survived by Annie, Herbert Williams' daughter. In her kindly company, amongst the portraits of her ancestors and the many relics of the decoy, in the manner in which she recalls the past with its sad, but more often happy, days, one can sense the pride she so justifiably feels in her family's long history and one in turn is proud to have been her friend.

List of birds recorded at Borough Fen Decoy. 1957-77

Tachybaptus ruficollis   Little Grebe   Breeds.
Podiceps cristatus   Gt. Crested Grebe   Regular Visitor.
Ardea cinerea   Heron   Regular Visitor.
Anas platyrhynchos   Mallard   Resident. Breeds.
Anas crecca   Teal   Winter visitor.
Anas querquedula   Garganey   Passage visitor.
Anas strepera   Gadwall   Passage visitor.
Anas penelope   Wigeon   Winter visitor.
Anas acuta   Pintail   Winter visitor.
Anas clypeata   Shoveler   Resident. Has bred
Aix galericulata   Mandarin   Feral.
Netta rufina   Red-crested Pochard   Three Winter records.
Aythya fuligula   Tufted Duck   Winter visitor. Bred once.
Aythya ferina   Pochard   Winter visitor.
Bucephala clangula   Goldeneye   One Winter record.
Tadorna tadorna   Shelduck   Occasional.
Anser brachyrhynchus   Pink-footed Goose   Winter visitor pre 1970
Branta canadensis   Canada Goose   Four records.
Cygnus olor   Mute Swan   Breeds every year.
Cygnus cygnus   Whooper Swan   Passage migrant.
Cygnus bewickii   Bewick's Swan   Passage migrant.
Buteo buteo   Buzzard   Passage migrant three records.
Accipiter nisus   Sparrow Hawk   Bred prior to 1960.
Falco peregrinus   Peregrine   One record May 1963.
Falco tinnunculus   Kestrel   Resident.
Alectoris rufa   Red-legged Partridge   Resident. Breeds.
Perdix perdix   English Partridge   Resident. Breeds.
Phasianus colchicus   Pheasant   Resident. Breeds.
Rallus aquaticus   Water Rail   Winter visitor.
Gallinula chloropus   Moorhen   Resident. Breeds.
Fulica atra   Coot   Winter visitor. Has bred.
Vanellus vanellus   Lapwing   Resident. Breeds nearby.
Pluvialis apricaria   Golden Plover   Winter visitor.
Charadrius dubius   Little Ringed Plover   Three records.
Gallinago gallinago   Snipe   Common Winter visitor.
Scolopax rustica   Woodcock   Autumn and Winter.
Numenius arquarta   Curlew   Passage. Spring and Autumn.
Tringa ochropus   Green Sandpiper   Autumn passage.
Actitis hypoleucos   Common Sandpiper   Autumn Passage.
Tringa stagnatilis   Marsh Sandpiper   One record April 1975.
Tringa erythropus   Spotted Redshank   Three records 1967-72-75.
Tringa totanus   Redshank   Regular Sept. to March.
Tringa nebularia   Greenshank   Autumn passage.
Philomachus pugnax   Ruff   Autumn passage.
Larus fuscus   Lesser Black-backed Gull   Irregular all year.
Larus marinus   Gtr. Black-backed Gull   Irregular all year.
Larus argentatus   Herring Gull   Common all year.
Larus ridibundus   Black-headed Gull   Common all year.
Sterna hirundo   Common Tern   Summer visitor. Breeds locally.
Columba oenas   Stock Dove   Resident. Breeds.
Columba palumbus   Wood Pigeon   Resident. Breeds.
Streptopelia turtur   Turtle Dove   Summer visitor. Breeds.
Streptopelia decaocto   Collard Dove   Resident.
Cuculus canorus   Cuckoo   Summer visitor. Breeds.
Tyto alba   Barn Owl   Regular. Breeds nearby.
Athene noctua   Little Owl   Regular. Breeds nearby.
Strix aluco   Tawny Owl   Resident. Breeds annually.
Asio otus   Long-eared Owl   Irregular. Bred 1960.
Asio flammeus   Short-eared Owl   Winter visitor.
Caprimulgus europaeus   Nightjar   One record. 1966.
Apus apus   Swift   Summer visitor. Non breeder.
Alcedo atthis   Kingfisher   Irregular resident. Has bred.
Upupa epops   Hoopoe   One record 1969.
Picus viridis   Green Woodpecker   Scarce since 1963.

Dendrocopus major   Gtr. Spotted Woodpecker   Resident. Breeds.
Dendrocopus minor   Lesser Spotted Woodpecker   One record 1974
Alaudia arvensis   Skylark   Very common in nearby fields.
Riparia riparia   Sand Martin   Summer visitor.
Dechilon urbica   House Martin   Summer visitor.
Hirunda rustica   Swallow   Summer visitor. Breeds.
Motacilla flava   Yellow Wagtail   Autumn passage.
Motacilla alba   Pied Wagtail   Resident. Breeds.
Anthus pratensis   Meadow Pipit   Irregular visitor.
Anthus trivialis   Tree Pipit   One record April 1973.
Corvus c. corone   Carrion Crow   Resident. Breeds.
Corvus c. cornix   Hooded Crow   Rare Winter visitor.
Corvus frugilegus   Rook   Bred before 1958. Common.
Corvus monedula   Jackdaw   Common. Has bred.
Pica pica   Magpie   Bred before 1970. Now scarce.
Garrulus glandarius   Jay   Bred before 1965. Now scarce.
Bombicilla garrulus   Waxwing   Winter visitor. 4 records.
Lanius excubitor   Great Grey Shrike   One record. Winter 1971/72.
Parus major   Great Tit   Resident. Breeds.
Parus caeruleus   Blue Tit   Resident. Breeds.
Parus montanus   Willow Tit   Resident. Breeds.
Parus palustris   Marsh Tit   One bird trapped.
Aegithalos caudatus   Long-tailed Tit   Resident. Breeds.
Certhia familiaris   Tree Creeper   Resident. Breeds.
Troglodytes troglodytes   Wren   Resident. Breeds.
Turdus torquatus   Ring Ouzel   Two records.
Turdus merula   Blackbird   Resident. Breeds.
Turdus pilaria   Fieldfare   Winter visitor.
Turdus iliacus   Redwing   Winter visitor.
Turdus philomelos   Song Thrush   Resident. Breeds.
Turdus viscivorus   Mistle Thrush   Resident. Breeds.
Oenanthe oenanthe   Wheatear   Passage migrant.
Phoenicurus phoenicurus   Redstart   Few records.
Phoenicurus ochrurus   Black Redstart   1 record March 1976.
Luscinia megarhynchos   Nightingale   Irregular. Has bred.
Erithacus rubecula   Robin   Resident. Breeds.
Locustella naevia   Grasshopper Warbler   Passage.
Acrocephalus scirpaceus   Reed Warbler   Summer visitor. Breeds.
Acrocephalus schoenbaenus   Sedge Warbler   Summer visitor.
Hippolais icterina   Icterine Warbler   One record. Trapped 1963.
Sylvia atricapilla   Blackcap   Summer visitor. Breeds.
Sylvia borin   Garden Warbler   Summer visitor. Breeds.
Sylvia communis   Whitethroat   Summer visitor. Breeds.
Sylvia curruca   Lesser Whitethroat   Summer visitor. Breeds.
Phylloscopus trochilus   Willow Warbler   Summer visitor. Breeds.
Phylloscopus collybita   Chiffchaff   Summer visitor. Breeds.
Muscicapa striata   Spotted Flycatcher   Summer visitor. Breeds.
Ficedula hypoleuca   Pied Flycatcher   Scarce. Attempted breeding
Regulus regulus   Goldcrest   Irregular visitor. Suspected breeding.
Prunella modularis   Dunnock   Resident. Breeds.
Sturnus vulgaris   Starling   Resident. Breeds.
Carduelis chloris   Greenfinch   Resident. Breeds.
Carduelis carduelis   Goldfinch   Resident. Breeds.
Carduelis spinus   Siskin   Irregular visitor.
Acanthis flammea   Lesser Redpoll   Bred annually since 1973.
Acanthis cannabina   Linnet   Resident. Breeds.
Pyrrhula pyrrhula   Bullfinch   Resident. Breeds.
Fringilla coecebs   Chaffinch   Resident. Breeds.
Fringilla montefringilla   Brambling   Winter visitor.
Emberiza calandra   Corn Bunting   Irregular. Has bred.
Emberiza citrinella   Yellowhammer   Resident. Breeds.
Emberiza schoeniclus   Reed Bunting   Resident. Breeds.
Passer domesticus   House Sparrow   Resident. Breeds.
Passer montanus   Tree Sparrow   Resident. Breeds.

APPENDIX B

List of plants recorded at Borough Fen Decoy
1969-74

Acer pseudoplatanus L.   Sycamore.
Aesculus hippocastanum L.   Horse Chestnut.
Agropyron repens L.   Twitch.
Agrostis stolonifera L.   Creeping Bent Grass.
Alisma plantago-aquatica L.   Water Plantain.
Alnus incana L.   Grey Alder.
Alnus glutinosa L.   Alder.
Alopecurus Myosuroides Huds.   Slender Fox-tail.
Alopecurus pratensis L.   Meadow Fox-tail.
Anemone nemorosa L.   Wood Anemone.
Anthriscus sylvestris L.   Cow Parsley.
Angelica sylvestris L.   Wild Angelica.
Aquilegia vulgaris Hoffm.   Columbine.
Arctium lappa L.   Great Burdock.
Arctium minus Bernh.   Lesser Burdock.
Arctium pubens Bab.   Common Burdock.
Armoracia rusticana Gaertn.   Horse Radish.
Arrhenathermum elatius Beauv.   Oat Grass.
Arum maculatum L.   Cuckoo-pint.
Bellis perennis L.   Daisy.
Berula erecta Corville.   Narrow-leaved Water Parsnip.
Betula pendula Roth.   Silver Birch.
Betula pubescens Ehrh.   Brown Birch.
Bromus mollis L.   Soft Brome.
Bromus sterilis L.   Barren Brome.

Bryonia dioica Jacq.   White Bryony.
Calamagrostis epigejos Roth.   Wood Small-reed.
Callitriche spp.   Water Starwort.
Caltha palustris L.   Marsh Marigold.
Calystegia sepium L.   Bindweed.
Capsela bursa pastoris L.   Shepherd's Purse.
Carduus acanthoides L.   Welted Thistle.
Carex acuta L.   Slender-spiked Sedge.
Carex acutiformis Ehrh.   Lesser Pond Sedge.
Carex obtrubae Podp.   False Fox Sedge.
Carex riparia Curt.   Great Pond Sedge.
Castenea sativa Mill.   Sweet Chestnut.
Ceratophyllum demersum L.   Hornwort.
Cerastium holosteoides Fr.   Common M'ouse-ear.
Centaurea nigra L.   Knapweed.
Chamaenerion angustifolium L.   Rosebay Willowherb.
Chrysanthemum parthenium Bernh.   Bachelor's Buttons.
Circaea lucetiana L.   Enchanter's Nightshade.
Cirsium arvense Scop.   Creeping Thistle.
Cirsium palustre Scop.   Marsh Thistle.
Cirsium vulgare Ten.   Spear Thistle.
Clematis vitalba L.   Old Man's Beard.
Conium maculatum L.   Hemlock.
Conopodium majus Gouan.   Pignut.
Convolvulus arvensis L.   Lesser Bindweed.

Coryllus avellana L. Hazel.
Crataegus monogyna Jacq. Common Hawthorn.
Dactylis glomerata. Cocksfoot.
Deschampsia caespitosa Beauv. Tufted Hair Grass.
Dryopteris filix-mas Schott. Male Fern.
Endymion hispanicus Mill. Bluebell.
Epilobium hirsutum. Great Willowherb.
Epilobium perviflorum Schreb. Hairy Willowherb.
Festuca gigantea Vill. Giant Fescue.
Festuca rubra L. Red Fescue.
Filipendula ulmaria L. Meadow Sweet.
Fraxinus excelsior L. Ash.
Galeobdolon luteum Huds. Yellow Archangel.
Galeopsis speciosa Mill. Large-leaved Hemp-nettle.
Galium aparine L. Goosegrass.
Galium uliginosum L. Fen Bedstraw.
Geranium dissectum L. Cut-leaved Cranesbill.
Geranium robertianum L. Herb Robert.
Geum rivale L. Water Avens.
Geum urbanum L. Wood Avens.
Glechoma hederacea L. Ground Ivy.
Glyceria maxima Holmberg. Reed Giant Grass.
Hedera Helix L. Ivy.
Heracleum sphondylium L. Hogweed.
Hesperis matronalis L. Dame's Violet.
Holcus lanatus L. Yorkshire Fog.
Hordeum Murium L. Wild Barley.
Humulus lupulus L. Hop.
Ilex aquifolium L. Holly.
Iris foetidissima L. Stinking Iris.
Iris pseudacorus L. Yellow Flag.
Juncus spp.
Knautia arvensis L. Field Scabious.
Lamium album L. White Dead-nettle.
Lamium purpureum L. Purple Dead-nettle.
Lapsana communis L. Nipple Wort.
Larix decidua Miller. Larch.
Lemna minor L. Small Duck-weed.
Lemna trisulca L. Ivy-leaved Duck-weed.
Ligustrum vulgare L. Privet.
Lolium perenne L. Rye Grass.
Lonicera periclymenum L. Honeysuckle.
Lysimachia nummularia L. Creeping Jenny.
Malus sylvestris Miller. Crab-apple.
Lychnis flos-cuculi L. Ragged Robin.
Malva neglecta Wallr. Dwarf Mallow.
Matricularia matricoides Porter. Wild cammomile.
Mahonia aquifolium. Oregon Grape.
Melandrium dioicum L. Red Campion.
Mercurialis perennis L. Dog's Mercury.
Moehringia trinervis Clairv. Three-veined Sandwort.
Myosotis arvensis Hill. Common Forget-me-not.
Myosotis scorpioides L. Water Forget-me-not.
Ornithogallum umbellatum L. Star of Bethlehem.
Papaver rhoeas L. Red Poppy.
Phleum pratense L. Timothy.
Phragmites communis Trin. Common Reed.
Picea abies Karsten. Norway Spruce.
Plantago lanceolata L. Ribwort Plantain.
Plantago major L. Greater Plantain.
Poa annua L. Annual Meadow Grass.
Poa pratense L. Meadow Grass.
Poa trivialis L. Rough Meadow Grass.
Polygonum persicaria L. Common Persicaria.
Populus alba L. White Poplar.
Populus canadensis Hartig. Hybrid Black Poplar.
Populus canescens Sm. Grey Poplar.
Potamogeton crispus L. Curled Pondweed.
Potamogeton natans L. Floating Pondweed.
Potentilla anserina L. Silver-weed.
Primula veris L. Cowslip.
Primula vulgaris Huds. Primrose.

Prunella vulgaris L. Self-heal
Prunus cerasus L. Dwarf Cherry.
Prunus lusitanica. Portugal Laurel.
Prunus spinosa L. Blackthorn.
Prunus domestica L. Wild plum.
Prunus interstitia L. Bullace.
Pyrus communis L. Pear.
Quercus robor L. Pedunculate Oak.
Quercus petraea Leebl. Sessile Oak.
Ranunculus L. bulbosus. Bulbous Buttercup.
Ranunculus repens L. Creeping Buttercup.
Ranunculus sceleratus L. Celery-leaved Crowfoot.
Ranunculus trichophyllus Chaix. Dark-hair Crowfoot.
Rorippa amphibia L. Amphibious Yellow Cress.
Rorippa nasturtium-aquaticum L. Water Cress.
Rosa spp.
Rubus fructicosus agg. Blackberry.
Rubus ulmifolius Schott.
Rumex acetosa L. Common Sorrel.
Rumex obtusifolius L. Broad-leaved Dock.
Rumex sanguineus L. Red-veined Dock.
Salix alba L. White Willow.
Salix atrocinerea Brot. Common Sallow.
Salix caprea L. Great or Goat Sallow.
Salix fragilis L. Crack Willow.
Salix pentandra L. Bay Willow.
Salix triandra L. Almond Willow.
Salix viminalis L. Common Osier.
Sambucus nigra L. Elder.
Sanicula europaea L. Sanicle.
Scrophularia aquatica L. Water Figwort.
Schrophularia nodosa L. Figwort.
Scutellaria galericulata L. Skull-cap.
Senecio jacobaea L. Ragwort.
Senecio vulgaris L. Groundsel.
Silene alba Mill. White Campion.
Sinapis arvensis L. Charlock.
Sonchus asper L. Prickly Sowthistle.
Sonchus oleracea L. Common Sowthistle.
Sorbus aucuparia L. Mountain Ash.
Stachys sylvatica L. Wood Woundwort.
Stellaria media L. Chickweed.
Symphytum officinale L. Comfrey.
Syringa vulgaris L. Lilac.
Tamus communis L. Black Bryony.
Taraxacum sect. officinale agg. Dandelions.
Taxus baccata L. Yew.
Tilia vulgaris. Common Lime.
Tussilago farfara L. Colt's foot.
Trifolium repens L. White Clover.
Ulmus glabra Huds. Wych Elm.
Ulmus procera Salisbury. English Elm.
Urtica dioica L. Stinging Nettle.
Urtica urens L. Small Nettle.
Veronica chamaedrys L. Germander Speedwell.
Viola odorata L. Sweet Violet.
Viola reichenbachiana Jord. ex Por. Woodland Violet.

Mosses.

Aula androgynum.
Brachythecium rutabulum.
Dicranoweissia cirrata.
Eurhynchium praelongum.
Fissidens taxifolius.
Hypnum cupressiforme.
Mnium undulatum.
Thamnium alopecurum.
Thumidium tamariscinum.

Liverwort.
Lophocolea bidentata.

APPENDIX C

LIST OF LEPIDOPTERA RECORDED AT
BOROUGH FEN DECOY 1954-1974

LEPIDOPTERA

Papilionidae.

Pieris brassicae L. Large Garden White.
Pieris rapae L. Small Garden White.
Pieris napi L. Green-veined White.
Anthocharis cardamines. Orange-tip.
Gonopteryx rhamni L. Brimstone.
Pararge megera L. Wall.
Pararge aegeria L. Speckled Wood.
Maniola jurtina L. Meadow Brown.
Maniola tithonus L. Gatekeeper.
Aphantopus hyperanthus L. Ringlet.
Lycaena phlaeas L. Small Copper.
Celastrinus argiolus L. Holly Blue.
Ochlodes venata Br. & G. Large Skipper.
Aglais Urticae, Small Tortoiseshell.
Vanessa Atlanta. Red Admiral.
Polygonia C-Album. Comma.
Inachis Io. Peacock.

Sphinges.

Mimas tiliae L. Lime Hawk.
Laothoe popula L. Poplar Hawk.
Smerinthus ocellata L. Eyed Hawk.
Sphinx ligustri L. Privet Hawk.

Bombyces

Harpyia bifida Brahm. Poplar Kitten.
Harpyia furcula Clerck. Sallow Kitten.
Cerura vinula L. Puss.
Pheosia tremula Clerck. Greater Swallow Prominent.
Pheosia gnoma F. Lesser Swallow Prominent.
Notodonta ziczac L. Pebble Prominent.
Notodonta dromedarius L. Iron Prominent.
Lophopteryx capucina L. Coxcomb Prominent.
Pterostoma palpina Clerck. Pale Prominent.
Phalera bucephala L. Buff-tip.

Hanrosyne pyritoides Hufn.   Buff Arches.
Thyatira batis L.   Peach Blossom.
Tethea ocularis L.   Figure of Eighty.
Tethea duplaris L.   Least Satin Lutestring.
Orgyia antiqua L.   Vapourer.
Dasychira pudibunda L.   Pale Tussock.
Euproctis similis Fuessl.   Gold-tail.
Malacosoma neustria L.   Common Lackey.
Philudoria potatoria L.   Drinker.
Cilix glaucata Scop.   Chinese Character.
Drepana binaria Hufn.   Oak Hook-tip.
Nola cucullatella L.   Short-cloaked.
Eilema lurideola Zinck.   Common Footman.
Eilema griseola Hubn.   Dingy Footman.
Spilosoma lubricipeda L.   White Ermine.
Spilosoma lutea Hufn.   Buff Ermine.
Cycnia mendica Clerck.   Muslin.
Phragmatobia fuliginosa L.   Ruby Tiger.
Arctia caia L.   Garden Tiger.

Noctuoidea

Euxoa nigricans L.   Garden Dart.
Euxua tritica L.   White-line Dart.
Agrotis segetum Schiff.   Turnip Dart.
Peridroma porphyrea Schiff.   Pearly Underwing.
Spaelotis ravida Schiff.   Stout Dart.
Graphiphora augug F.   Double Dart.
Diarsia mendica F.   Ingrailed Clay.
Diarsia brunnea Fabr.   Purple Clay.
Diarsia rubi View.   Small Square-spot.
Amathes c-nigrum L.   Setaceous Hebrew Character.
Amathes triangulum Hufn.   Double Square-spot.
Amathes sexstrigata Haw.   Six-striped Rustic.
Amathes xanthographa Schiff.   Square-spot Rustic.
Ochropleura plecta L.   Flame Shoulder.
Axtlia putris L.   Flame Rustic.
Triphaena comes Hubn.   Lesser Yellow-underwing.
Triphaena janthina.   Lesser Broad-bordered Yellow Underwing
Dampra fimbriata Screb.   Broad-bordered Yellow-underwing.
Pyrrhia umbra Hufn.   Bordered Orange.
Mamestra brassicae L.   Cabbage.
Melanchra persicariae L.   White Dot.
Polia nitens Haw.   Pale Shining Brown.
Ceramica pisi L.   Broom.
Diataraxa oleracea L.   Bright-line Brown-eye.
Hadena thalassina Hufn.   Pale-shouldered Brocade.
Hadena bicruris Hufn.   Lychnis.
Hadena rivularis F.   Campion.
Hadena dolorata Hufn.   Broad-barred White.
Scotogramma trifolii. Hufn.   Small Nutmeg.
Heliophobus reticulata Vill.   Bordered Gothic.
Tholera popularis F.   Feathered Gothic.
Tholera cespitis Schiff.   Hedge Rustic.
Cerapteryx graminis L.   Antler.
Orthosia gothica L.   Hebrew Character.
Orthosia cruda Schiff.   Small Quaker.
Orthosia stabilis Schiff.   Common Quaker.
Orthosia populeti F.   Lead-coloured Drab.
Orhtosia incerta Hufn.   Clouded Drab.
Orthosia gracilis Schiff.   Powdered Quaker.
Leucania pallens. L.   Common Wainscot.
Leucania impura Hubn.   Smoky Wainscot.
Leucania obsoleta Hubn.   Obscure Wainscot.
Leucania comma L.   Shoulder-striped Wainscot.
Leucania lithargyria Esp.   Clay Wainscot.
Leucania conigera Schiff.   Brown-line Wainscot.
Rhizedra lutosa Hubn.   Large Wainscot.
Arenostola phragmitidis Hubn.   Fen Wainscot.
Nonagria dissoluta Treits.   Brown-veined Wainscot.
Chilodes maritima Tausch.   Silky Wainscot.
Meristis trigrammica Hufn.   Treble-lines.
Caradrina morpheus Hufn.   Mottles Rustic.
Caradrina alsines Brahm.   Uncertain.
Caradrina clavipalpis Scop.   Pale Mottled Willow.
Apamea sordens Hufn.   Rustic Shoulder-knot.
Apamea unanimis Hubn.   Small Clouded Brindle.
Apamea secalis L.   Common Rustic.
Apamea ophiogramma Esp.   Double-lobed.
Apamea crenata Hufn.   Clouded-bordered Brindle.
Apamea remissa Hubn.   Dusky Brindle.
Apamea monoglypha Hufn.   Dark Arches.
Procus strigilis Clerck.   Marbled minor.
Procus fasciuncula Haw.   Middle-barred Minor.
Procus latruncula Schiff.   Tawny Minor.
Procus furuncula Schiff.   Cloaked Minor.
Luperina testacea Schiff.   Flounced Rustic.
Euplexia lucipara L.   Small Angle-shades.
Phlogophora meticulosa L.   Large Angle-shades.
Petilampa minima Hufn.   Small Dotted Buff.
Hydraecia oculea L.   Common Ear.
Gortyna flavago Schiff.   Orange Ear.
Gortyna micacea Esp.   Rosy Ear.
Cosmia affinis L.   Lesser Spotted Pinion.
Cosmia trapezina L.   Dunbar.
Zenobia subtusa Schiff.   Olive.

Amphipyra tragopogonis Clerck.   Mouse.
Rusina tenebrosa Hubn.   Brown Feathered Rustic.
Apatele megacephala Schiff.   Poplar Grey.
Apatele rumicis L.   Knot-grass.
Apatele psi. L.   Grey Dagger.
Cryphia perla Schiff.   Marbled Beau.
Cucullia umbratica L.   Shark.
Lithophane semibrunnea Haw.   Tawny Pinion.
Xylocampa areola Esp.   Early Grey.
Bombycia viminalis F.   Minor Shoulder-knot.
Allophyes oxyacanthae L.   Green-brindled Crescent.
Fumichtis adusta Esp.   Dark Brocade.
Antitype flavicincta Schiff.   Large Ranunculus.
Eupsilia transversa Esp.   Satellite.
Agrochola circillaris Hufn.   Brick.
Agrochola lychnidis Schiff.   Beaded Chestnut. ·
Agrochola macilenta Hubn.   Yellow-lined Quaker.
Citria lutea Strohm.   Pink-barred Sallow.
Cirrhia icteritia Hufn.   Sallow.
Cirrhia icteritia Hufn.   Sallow.
Cirrhia gilvago Schiff.   Dusky-lemon Sallow.
Bena prasinana L.   Green Silver-lines.
Earias clorana L.   Cream-bordered Pea.
Lithacodia fasciana L.   White Marbled.
Catocala nupta L.   Red Underwing.
Episema caeruleocephala L.   Figure of Eight.
Plusia chrysitis L.   Burnished Brass.
Plusia iota L.   Plain Golden-Y.
Plusia pulchrina L.   Beautiful Golden-Y.
Plusia gamma L.   Silver-Y.
Unca triplasia L.   Dark Spectacle.
Unca tripartita Hufn.   Light Spectacle.
Scoliopteryx libatrix L.   Herald.
Hypena proboscidalis L.   Common Snout.
Zanclognatha nemoralis F.   Small Fanfoot.
Laspeyria flexula Schiff.   Beautiful Hook-wing.

Geometridae.

Jodis lactearia L.   Little Emerald.
Hemithea aestivaria Hubn.   Common Emerald.
Sterrha traminata Borkh.   Plain Wave.
Sterrha aversata L.   Riband Wave.
Sterrha biselata Hufn.   Small Fan-footed Wave.
Scopula Immutata L.   Lesser Cream Wave.
Scopula imitaria Hubn.   Small Blood-vein.
Scopula lactata Haw.   Greater Cream Wave.
Calothysanis amata L.   Blood-vein.
Lobophora halterata Hufn.   Seraphim.
Ecliptoptera silaceata Schiff.   Small Phoenix.
Xanthorhoe quadrifasiata Clerck.   Large Twin-spot Carpet.
Xanthorhoe ferrugata Clerck.   Dark-barred Twin-spot.
Xanthorhoe spadicearia Schiff.   Red Twin-spot.
Xanthorhoe montanata Borkh.   Silver-ground Carpet.
Xanthorhoe fluctuata L.   Garden Carpet.
Colostygia pectinataria Knoch.   Green Carpet.
Colostygia didymata L.   Small Twin-spot Carpet.
Dysstroma truncata Hufn.   Common Marbled Carpet.
Euphyia bilineata L.   Yellow Shell.
Hydriomena furcata Thunb.   July Highflyer.
Epirrhoe alternata Mull.   Bedstraw Carpet.
Pelurga comitata L.   Dark Spinach.
Plemyria rubiginata Schiff.   Blue-bordered Carpet.
Oporinia dilutata Schiff.   November Carpet.
Eupithecia. centaureata Schiff.   Lime-speck Pug.
Eupithecia exiguata Hubn.   Mottled Pug.
Eupithecia absinthiata Clerck.   Wormwood Pug.
Eupithecia vulgata Haw.   Common Pug.
Eupithecia succenturiata L.   Bordered Pug.
Eupithecia icterata Vill.   Tawny-speckled Pug.
Chloroclystis coronata Hubn.   V-Pug.
Chloroclystis rectangulata L.   Green Pug.
Abraxas grossulariata L.   Magpie.
Lomaspilis marginata L.   Clouded Border.
Bapta temerata Hubn.   Clouded Silver.
Bapta bimaculata F.   White-spotted Pinion.
Deilinia pusaria L.   White Wave.
Deilinia exanthemata Scop.   Common Wave.
Erannis marginaria F.   Dotted Border.
Erannis defoliaria Clerck.   Mottled Umber.
Deuteronomis alniaria L.   Canary-shouldered Thorn.
Deuteronomos fuscantaria Haw.   Dusky Thorn.
Selenia bilunaria Esp.   Early Thorn.
Gonodontis bidentata Clerck.   Scalloped Hazel.
Crocallis elinguaria L.   Scalloped Oak.
Colotois pennaria L.   Feathered Thorn.
Ourapteryx sambucaria L.   Swallow-tailed.
Biston betularia L.   Peppered Moth.
Cleora rhomboidaria Schiff.   Willow Beauty.
Ectropis crepuscularia Hubn.   Small Engrailed.
Chiasmia clathrata L.   Latticed Heath.

Psychoidea

Sesia bembeciformis Hubn.   Osier Hornet Clearwing.
Aegeria formicaeformis Esp.   Red-tipped Clearwing.

64